EDITH HAMILTON has won a notable place in contemporary American letters through her books on the culture of the ancient world. A student of the classics from her earliest youth, she read Latin and Greek all her life for her own pleasure. She was graduated from Bryn Mawr in 1894 and did graduate work in Greek and Latin at the University of Munich, to which she was the first woman ever admitted. She was for twenty-five years Head Mistress of the Bryn Mawr School for Girls in Baltimore. It was not until 1930, when she was 63, that she began her writing career with *The Greek Way*. At once Miss Hamilton won a wide and ardent audience. That audience has been augmented with each of her subsequent books: *The Roman Way, Spokesmen for God, Three Greek Plays, Mythology, Witness to the Truth,* and *The Echo of Greece*.

Books by Edith Hamilton

THE GREEK WAY

THE ROMAN WAY

THREE GREEK PLAYS

MYTHOLOGY

WITNESS TO THE TRUTH

SPOKESMEN FOR GOD

THE ECHO OF GREECE

❧ The ❧
EVER-PRESENT
PAST

by

EDITH HAMILTON

PROLOGUE BY DORIS FIELDING REID

COPYRIGHT © 1964 BY
W. W. Norton & Company Inc.

First published in the Norton Library 1987

All Rights Reserved

Published simultaneously in Canada by
George J. McLeod Limited, Toronto

Books That Live

The Norton imprint on a book means that in the publisher's
estimation it is a book not for a single season but for the years.

The Norton Library
W · W · NORTON & COMPANY · INC ·
NEW YORK

Printed in the United States of America

ISBN 0 393 00425 2

COPYRIGHT © 1964 BY
W. W. Norton & Company, Inc.

First published in the Norton Library 1967

Books That Live
The Norton imprint on a book means that in the publisher's
estimation it is a book not for a single season but for the years.

W. W. NORTON & COMPANY, INC.

Printed in the United States of America
3 4 5 6 7 8 9

CONTENTS

PROLOGUE

Written Shortly Before Edith Hamilton's
Sudden Death

Shortly after Edith Hamilton's 92nd birthday, we were called upon by an English actress who was putting on Edith's translation of the *Agamemnon* of Aeschylus. She wanted to know if Edith could be persuaded to translate the rest of the *Oresteia*. "No" said Edith, and then added, "I am saving translating for my old age." She said this with a smile but she meant it and in the presence of her extraordinary power and vitality of mind and body, her remark somehow seemed quite reasonable. This power and vitality has been one of her outstanding characteristics all her life.

I was a pupil in the Bryn Mawr School in Baltimore when Edith was Head Mistress. Baltimore in those days—the early 1900's—was essentially a southern city where girls were not supposed to learn anything in particular. But Bryn Mawr was not that kind of a school at all. In a recent anniversary bulletin of the Bryn Mawr School, Edith wrote the following "Message":

"It is over half a century since I came to the Bryn Mawr School. The school was then the only strictly college preparatory school for girls in the United States. All the others had a non-college-preparatory course which was notably easier. Our school was the hardest and from the moment I became its head I took great pride in that. The idea that we might be causing inferiority complexes never occurred to me. The notion had not yet invaded school precincts and my own experience, far from leading me to it, made me convinced that the Bryn Mawr College entrance examinations could be passed by every girl who was willing to work hard, very hard in some cases, I admit.

"But it is not hard work which is dreary; it is superficial work. That is always boring in the long run, and it has always seemed strange to me that in our endless discussions about education so little stress is ever laid on the pleasure of becoming an educated person, the enormous interest it adds to life.

"I got a great deal of fun out of teaching Virgil. I remember once translating to my class the description in the *Aeneid* of the exhausted oarsmen after the great boat race. Here a tribute is due to the lovely manners of the Baltimore girls which were always a pleasure to me. In this particular instance they listened to me without even so much as a smile. In the next number of the school magazine there appeared: 'One whose words we always revere tells us that *"Anhelitus quatit membra"* should be translated, "Their limbs shook from their pants."'

"The atmosphere of the school was not dull or depressing. Again and again I saw that delightful thing, an awakening to the joys of knowledge. I became convinced that real education was a matter of individual conversion and the result was that I loved teaching far and away more than anything else I did."

Edith made the most academically difficult girls' school in the United States the most popular school in Baltimore, a city where many of the parents not only did not care whether their daughters learned anything or not, but in some cases, felt it a great mistake for them to do so.

What was her secret? It was partly her power and vitality of mind. The school was always alive and interesting. One of my classmates wrote me "Nothing was ever *dull* with Miss Hamilton around," but that was not the whole of it. Years ago one of her alumnae wrote "A Tribute" that put into words what all of us felt. The following is taken from it:

"Miss Hamilton—even to the younger children, before we had entered the lighted circle of her classes—was a figure of high, mysterious power. When she slipped into the study hall, and took up her place at the desk, to read or mark papers, her mind remote from us and our infinitesimal concerns, the buzz and rattle of the ordinary regime sank to perfect stillness; and a hush ever followed her swift passage as she swept by us on the stairs.

"I think I do not exaggerate, or speak only for myself, when I say that she brought in with her the air of having come from some high centre of civilization, where the skies were loftier, the views more spacious, the atmosphere more free and open than with us.

"And to many of us she was the means of a higher gift than culture. Even a heedless school girl is aware, if dimly, of a noble and religious nature."

Edith retired from Bryn Mawr School in 1922 and the alumnae had a portrait painted of her. In acknowledging it she said, "This only bears out what I have been trying to teach you, and that is to look a plain fact in the face."

One of her alumnae said to me recently, "It is astonishing but Edith never changes. When I was at the school, some fifty years ago, her hair was brown; now it is white. Otherwise she is the same." There was, however, a change after she left the school, she was no longer a "Head Mistress," which was enormously freeing. An old friend of ours has just written me, "The minute Edith retired from the school she came out from her remoteness to become warmly accessible as a personality. Such is her agelessness that anyone, young or old, who knows her soon thinks of her as Edith, and calls her just that."

Several years after she left Baltimore she started on a new and what turned out to be her real career. Her first book was published in 1930.

What made her start writing is of interest and shows a quality of humility which is, I think, illuminating. In the early 1920's a small group of intimate friends were sitting around her tea table and one of them said "Edith, tell us something about the Greek tragedians. I really don't know the difference between Aeschylus, Sophocles and Euripides." "My *dear child!*" Edith exclaimed with fire in her eyes. She jumped up, got down her volume of the Greek plays and translated bits from each of the poets. She then started talking about and explaining Aeschylus, the tragedian she cared most for. Suddenly she said rather wistfully, "Oh, I am so afraid you don't like Aeschylus." There was a burst of laughter, and one of us said, "She talks about Aeschylus exactly as though he were her eldest son!" Another remarked, "She made me feel she must just have had lunch with him!"

From then on our little group met regularly to prod Edith with questions on almost every subject conceivable. After one discussion concerning the idea of tragedy, an editor of the *Theatre Arts Monthly* Magazine, who was one of our group, said, "Edith must write it all down and send it in to the magazine." Edith said she had never written and did not think that she could. Much urging and beseeching ensued. Finally, truly disturbed, Edith said, "*Please* do not press me so. How would you feel if I were imploring you to attempt to become an opera singer?" But the pressure continued and finally after some weeks the article was written and Edith's important and unique talent was instantly recognized.

After several of her articles on the Greek playwrights had appeared in the *Theatre Arts Monthly,* a publisher spotted "a real writer" and asked her to do a book for him on Greece. She immediately said she wouldn't and couldn't. She told him to go to the public library where he would find file drawer after file drawer listing books on Greece. What could she possibly say that hadn't already been said? She then told him what folly it would be for his firm to publish a book on Greece by an unknown writer, in no way recognized as a Greek scholar, and not even a professor in a university. She mustered her arguments and with her usual intensity threw herself into an attempt to dissuade him from trying to get her to write a book. But he persisted. He brought her a contract. She refused to sign it, saying it would be unfair to him to commit himself to publish what she might write. But he persisted. In the end he won. The book was written and *The Greek Way* was published in 1930. It received instant acclaim and its popularity grew steadily. In the 1940's it was published in a paperback edition and by now it is thought of as a classic.

Not long ago some one asked Edith what made her start writing. "I was bullied into it!" she answered truthfully.

As the years have gone on and her books and articles continue to appear, endless people have asked me such questions as: Where did she write? How long did she write a day? Did she dictate or write in longhand? etc. A reporter who was about to interview her once said to me, "I think I can just see her sitting upright at her desk producing a manuscript as neat and finished as she herself looks." What this young man thought he could "see" was about as far from reality as anything could possibly be. Edith always writes sitting in an arm chair with a pad, or any bit of paper she can lay her hands on, in her lap. Frequently the backs of envelopes are pressed into service. She writes everything in longhand. She scratches out; rewrites over passages only partially rubbed out; puts inserts on the margins, and the result is something next to illegible. The idea of copying it over so that a secretary can read it, bores Edith almost beyond endurance.

She is very fond of cooking and occasionally writes down recipes. These are also put on bits of paper or old envelopes. This has caused some difficulties. When she sent her translation of one of the Greek plays to her publisher, an agitated secretary called me up and said that there was something she could not understand. Right after the first chorus was a paragraph headed "Onion soup for four."

The numbering of her pages also presents a problem. She will be absorbed in what she is writing and after finishing, say, page 2, she will write 2 at the top of the next bit of paper. A friend of ours once said to me, "I just went up to see Edith and the whole room was covered with page 11."

To these little idiosyncrasies was added a further complication. Her kindliness and sense of responsibility often led her to employ secretaries so inept that she feared, and rightly, that no one else would possibly give them a job.

How does this description of her method of writing fit in with her published works which are noted for their finish and clarity? "Her finely chiseled prose" as one critic commented. Another critic wrote, "Her style is Doric in its simplicity, its strength, its beauty." I think the explanation is that she feels it is of no importance or interest how she writes, or where or on what. She throws her whole mind and heart into an effort to put into words what she profoundly believes. She often quotes an early Greek poet, "Before the gates of excellence the high gods have placed sweat." I think she has achieved excellence and before that gate I know she has placed sweat. She has never "tossed off" anything.

She has a power of concentration beyond that of anyone I have ever known. Authors, scientists, anyone doing original work inevitably requires a certain number of specified, uninterrupted hours set aside for their project. It takes a bit of time just to settle down and get started. Not so Edith! Hundreds of times I have known her, after chatting idly with the family, say, "Dinner will not be ready for fifteen minutes; I think I will do some work." She will get up, turn off her hearing aid, go to her chair beside the window and before she has even sat down, it is clear that her mind is completely concentrated and the whole outside world blotted out. Her one and only physical disability, that of being hard of hearing, has an occasional advantage. She can tune off.

We have a house on the rocks by the ocean in Maine, where for many years an assortment of nieces and nephews spent their summers. Edith would go sailing and picnicking and do all the cooking, but often on the rocky beach, after lunch was over, she would move a few feet away from the general pandemonium that only small children can produce, pull a pencil out of her pocket and settle down to write. When it seemed time to go, she tucked her pencil and paper away, but at home she could start again wherever she left off. It seems that she carries her detachment and absorption around with her and can drop into her inner sanctum at any moment she chooses.

Her phenomenal verbal memory doubtless plays its part in her ability to pick up quickly wherever she happens to leave off in her writing. One can hardly mention a poem that she does not know by heart. She once recited the whole of "Horatius at the Bridge" to some of the children up in Maine. Surprisingly her memory is not confined to poetry. I have often heard her quote paragraphs of prose. One of our friends said to me, "When Edith talks of some distinguished figure in the past, she does not tell me what he thought, she quotes exactly what he said." Edith always opened the Bryn Mawr School with a brief reading, usually from the Psalms or Gospels. I can see her now, an erect, distinguished figure, standing at the end of the long study hall, with a Bible open in her hand. But none of us can remember her ever looking at it.

Over the years Edith has received honorary degrees and various awards including The Gold Cross of the Legion of Benefaction from King Paul of Greece. But the honor she most deeply cared about was when she was made a citizen of Athens.

In the summer of 1957 the Greek government invited her to Athens as its guest to attend a performance of her translation of the *Prometheus* of Aeschylus. It took place in the theatre of Herodes Atticus at the foot of the Acropolis. This open-air amphitheatre holding 4,000 was packed and the audience seemed to extend right up into the skies.

When Edith came in there was a thunder of applause. With an amused and interested smile she was looking around to see for whom they were clapping when the Mayor of Athens, who was escorting her, leaned down and said:

"Bow, Miss Hamilton, *bow*. The applause is for *you*." He then led her onto the stage and after a citation, presented her with a scroll which made her a citizen of Athens. She in turn stepped to the microphone and made a brief speech that was somehow extraordinarily moving. *The New York Times* correspondent, describing the event, wrote, "The crowd showed itself to be moved by Miss Hamilton's appearance. In a brief speech she referred to freedom as a Greek discovery. . . . The ninety-year-old white haired author was the evening's leading attraction and what followed her appearance on the stage seemed anticlimactic."

Her vast number of friends and close acquaintances are to be found in every generation. "She means so much to so many people," someone once said of her. A friend remarked, "Edith is such fun, I love to see that twinkle come into her eyes because I know she is about to say something witty and probably a little wicked." Her wit and power of penetrating criticism are shown in many of her articles and book reviews. Some years ago she wrote of an eminent scholar's book on Greece that the enormous importance of ancient Greece has been "softly dimmed by the dust of scholarly elucidation." That sentence has been referred to many times, in praise and in rage. Her articles and essays have given much entertainment and edification. They show a range of interest and breadth of knowledge that would be surprising to those who know her only through her books.

A distinguished man of letters said to me: "She has a power of presentation, interpretation and illumination beyond that of any writer I know." Edith said after describing Thucydides' picture of the Athenians, "Only an ideal? Ideals have enormous power. They stamp an age, they lift up when they are lofty; they drag down and make decadent when they are low—and then, by that strange fact, the survival of the fittest, those that are low, fade away and are forgotten. The Greek ideals have had a power of persistent life for twenty-five hundred years." "The Excellent becomes the permanent," Aristotle said.

In the radio program "This I Believe" she said: "When the world we are living in is storm-driven and the bad that happens and the worst that threatens press urgently upon us, there is a strong tendency to emphasize men's baseness or their impotent insignificance. Is this the way the world is to go or not? It depends upon us.

"St. John spoke of the true light that lighteth every man coming into the world. Belief in the indestructible power of that light makes it indestructible. This lifts up the life of every man to an overwhelming importance and dignity."

John Mason Brown wrote of what he called the Hamilton Clubs which he found in "one American town after another" throughout the country, "that happily unorganized band of men and women whose eyes brighten at the merest mention of Edith." Of her book *Witness to the Truth* he wrote "I put it down the wiser, the more awakened, the more curious and the firmer in faith. I put it down, too, understanding why it is that those eyes brighten and strangers become friends at the merest mention of Edith Hamilton's name."

When she received an honorary degree at Yale University the citation referred to the "sheer power" of her books and said "your scholarly love of Greek culture is no repining for a dead past, but a new dimension of depth and beauty for our own civilization."

I think that all her readers will agree that her philosophy, her indomitable spirit, her deep and unshakable convictions come through all her works. They have what Schopenhauer describes as "That singular swing toward elevation."

DORIS FIELDING REID

March 15, 1963

ACKNOWLEDGMENTS

"Prologue" by Doris Fielding Reid appeared in *Greek Heritage*, Vol. 1, No. 1, Winter 1963. Copyright © 1963 by the Athenian Corporation. Reprinted by permission.

"The Ever-Present Past" appeared under the title "The Lessons of the Past" in *The Saturday Evening Post*, September 27, 1958, © 1958 The Curtis Publishing Company. Reprinted by permission.

"Plato" was an address given before the Classical Association of the Atlantic States, April 29, 1960. Previously unpublished.

"The Greek Chorus: Fifteen or Fifty?" appeared in *Theatre Arts Monthly*, June 1933. Copyright 1933 by Theatre Arts, Inc. Reprinted by permission.

"Comedy" appeared in *Theatre Arts Monthly*, July 1927. Copyright 1927 by Theatre Arts, Inc. Reprinted by permission.

"Tragedy As They Order It In France" appeared in *Theatre Arts Monthly*, September 1937. Copyright 1937 by Theatre Arts, Inc. Reprinted by permission.

"Goethe and Faust" appeared in a shortened version in *Theatre Arts Monthly*, June 1941. Copyright 1941 by Theatre Arts, Inc. Reprinted by permission.

"The World of Plato," a review of Werner Jaeger's *Paideia*, translated by Gilbert Highet appeared in *The New York Times Book Review*, January 2, 1944. Copyright 1944 by The New York Times Company. Reprinted by permission.

"Born Under a Rhyming Planet," a review of *The Seven Against Thebes* by Aeschylus, translated by Gilbert Murray, appeared in *Saturday Review*, June 29, 1935. Copyright 1935 by Saturday Review Associates, Inc. Reprinted by permission.

"A Tottering World," a review of *The Age of Constantine the Great* by Jakob Burckhardt, translated by Moses Hadas, appeared in *The New York Times Book Review*, September 4,

ACKNOWLEDGMENTS

1949. Copyright 1949 by The New York Times Company. Reprinted by permission.

"Word From New Zion," a review of Martin Buber's *Israel and the World*, appeared in *Saturday Review*, July 4, 1953. Copyright 1953 by Saturday Review Associates, Inc. Reprinted by permission.

"This Will Never Do" appeared in *The Saturday Review of Literature*, December 31, 1932. Copyright 1932 by Saturday Review Associates, Inc. Reprinted by permission.

"These Sad Young Men" appeared in *The Atlantic Monthly*, May 1929. Copyright 1929 by The Atlantic Monthly Company. Reprinted by permission.

"Private Idiom" appeared in *Vogue*, September 15, 1951. Copyright 1951, The Condé Nast Publications Inc. Reprinted by permission.

"Words, Words, Words" appeared in *Saturday Review*, November 19, 1955. Copyright 1955 by Saturday Review Associates, Inc. Reprinted by permission.

"William Faulkner" appeared under the title "Faulkner: Sorcerer or Slave?" in *Saturday Review*, July 12, 1952. Copyright 1952 by Saturday Review Associates, Inc. Reprinted by permission.

"The Way of the Church" was an address given at the Church of St. John, Washington, D.C. in 1960. Previously unpublished.

"This I Believe" appeared under the title "Of Sonnets, Symphonies and Socrates" in *This I Believe*, Second Series, written for Edward R. Murrow, edited by Raymond Swing, Simon and Schuster, New York, 1954. Copyright 1954 by Help, Inc. Reprinted by permission.

"Roots of Freedom," a radio address written for the Voice of America Roots of Freedom Series, appeared in *Greek Heritage*, Vol. 1, No. 1, Winter 1963. Copyright © 1963 by the Athenian Corporation. Reprinted by permission.

"Address to the Athenians" appeared under the title "The True Light" in *Saturday Review*, October 19, 1957. Copyright 1957 by Saturday Review Associates, Inc. Reprinted by permission.

The
EVER-PRESENT PAST

THE
EVER-PRESENT
PAST

Is there an ever-present past? Are there permanent truths which are forever important for the present? Today we are facing a future more strange and untried than any other generation has faced. The new world Columbus opened seems small indeed beside the illimitable distances of space before us, and the possibilities of destruction are immeasurably greater than ever. In such a position can we afford to spend time on the past? That is the question I am often asked. Am I urging the study of the Greeks and Romans and their civilizations for the Atomic Age?

Yes, that is just what I am doing. I urge it without qualifications. We have a great civilization to save—or to lose. The greatest civilization before ours was the Greek. They challenge us and we need the challenge. They, too, lived in a dangerous world. They were a little, highly civilized people, the only civilized people in the west, surrounded by barbarous tribes and with the greatest Asiatic power, Persia, always threatening them. In the end they succumbed, but the reason they did was not that the enemies outside were so strong, but that their own strength, their spiritual strength, had given way. While they had it they kept Greece unconquered and they left behind a record in art and thought which in all the centuries of human effort since has not been surpassed.

The point which I want to make is not that their taste was superior to ours, not that the Parthenon was their idea of church architecture, nor that Sophocles was the great drawing card in the theatres, nor any of the familiar comparisons between fifth-century Athens and twentieth-century America, but that Socrates found on every street corner and in every Athenian equivalent of the baseball field people who were caught up by his questions into the world of thought. To be able to be caught up into the world of thought—that is to be educated.

How is that great aim to be reached? For years we have eagerly discussed ways and means of education and the discussion still goes on. William James once said that there were two subjects which if mentioned made other conversation stop and directed all eyes to the speaker. Religion was one and education the other. Today Russia seems to come first, but education is still emphatically the second. In spite of all the articles we read and all the speeches we listen to about it, we want to know more; we feel deeply its importance.

There is today a clearly visible trend toward making it the aim of education to defeat the Russians. That would be a sure way to defeat education. Genuine education is possible only when people realize that it has to do with persons, not with movements.

When I read educational articles it often seems to me

that this important side of the matter, the purely personal side, is not emphasized enough—the fact that it is so much more agreeable and interesting to be an educated person than not. The sheer pleasure of being educated does not seem to be stressed. Once long ago I was talking with Professor Basil L. Gildersleeve of Johns Hopkins University, the greatest Greek scholar our country has produced. He was an old man and he had been honored everywhere, in Europe as well as in America. He was just back from a celebration held for him in Oxford. I asked him what compliment received in his long life had pleased him most. The question amused him and he laughed over it, but he thought too. Finally he said, "I believe it was when one of my students said, 'Professor, you have so much fun with your own mind.'" Robert Louis Stevenson said that a man ought to be able to spend two or three hours waiting for a train at a little country station when he was all alone and had nothing to read, and not be bored for a moment.

What is the education which can do this? What is the furniture which makes the only place belonging absolutely to each one of us, the world within, a place where we like to go? I wish I could answer that question. I wish I could produce a perfect decorator's design warranted to make any interior lovely and interesting and stimulating; but, even if I could, sooner or later we would certainly try different designs. My point is only that while we must and should change the furniture, we ought to throw away old furniture very cautiously. It may turn out to be irreplaceable. A great deal was thrown away in the last generation or so, long enough ago to show some of the results. Furniture which had for centuries been foremost, we lightly, in a few years, discarded. The classics almost vanished from our field of education. That was a great change. Along with it came another. There is a marked difference between the writers of the past and the writers of today who have been educated without benefit of Greek and Latin. Is this a matter of cause and effect? People will decide for themselves, but I do not think anyone will question the statement that clear thinking is not the characteristic which distinguishes our literature today. We are more and more caught up by the unintelligible. People like it. This argues an inability to think, or, almost as bad, a disinclination to think.

Neither disposition marked the Greeks. They had a passion for thinking things out, and they loved unclouded clarity of statement as well as of thought. The Romans did, too, in their degree. They were able to put an idea into an astonishingly small number of words without losing a particle of intelligibility. It is only of late, with a generation which has never had to deal with a Latin sentence, that we are being submerged in a flood of words, words, words. It has been said that Lincoln at Gettysburg today would have begun in some such fashion as this: "Eight and seven-tenths decades ago the pioneer workers in this continental area implemented a new group based on an ideology of free boundaries and initial equality," and might easily have ended, "That political supervision of the integrated units, for the integrated units, by the integrated units, shall not become null and void on the superficial area of this planet." Along with the banishment of the classics, gobbledygook has come upon us—and the appalling size of the *Congressional Record*, and the overburdened mail service.

Just what the teaching in the schools was which laid the

foundation of the Greek civilization we do not know in detail; the result we do know. Greek children were taught, Plato said, to "love what is beautiful and hate what is ugly." When they grew up their very pots and pans had to be pleasant to look at. It was part of their training to hate clumsiness and awkwardness; they loved grace and practiced it. "Our children," Plato said, "will be influenced for good by every sight and sound of beauty, breathing in, as it were, a pure breeze blowing to them from a good land."

All the same, the Athenians were not, as they showed Socrates when he talked to them, preoccupied with enjoying lovely things. The children were taught to think. Plato demanded a stiff examination, especially in mathematics, for entrance to his Academy. The Athenians were a thinking people. Today the scientists are bearing away the prize for thought. Well, a Greek said that the earth went around the sun sixteen centuries before Copernicus thought of it. A Greek said if you sailed out of Spain and kept to one latitude, you would come at last to land, seventeen hundred years before Columbus did it. Darwin said, "We are mere schoolboys in scientific thinking compared to old Aristotle." And the Greeks did not have a great legacy from the past as our scientists have; they thought science out from the beginning.

The same is true of politics. They thought that out, too, from the beginning, and they gave all the boys a training to fit them to be thinking citizens of a free state that had come into being through thought.

Basic to all the Greek achievement was freedom. The Athenians were the only free people in the world. In the great empires of antiquity—Egypt, Babylon, Assyria, Persia—splendid though they were, with riches beyond reckoning and immense power, freedom was unknown. The idea of it never dawned in any of them. It was born in Greece, a poor little country, but with it able to remain unconquered no matter what manpower and what wealth were arrayed against her. At Marathon and at Salamis overwhelming numbers of Persians had been defeated by small Greek forces. It had been proved that one free man was superior to many submissively obedient subjects of a tyrant. Athens was the leader in that amazing victory, and to the Athenians freedom was their dearest possession. Demosthenes said that they would not think it worth their while to live if they could not do so as free men, and years later a great teacher said, "Athenians, if you deprive them of their liberty, will die."

Athens was not only the first democracy in the world, it was also at its height an almost perfect democracy—that is, for men. There was no part in it for women or foreigners or slaves, but as far as the men were concerned it was more democratic than we are. The governing body was the Assembly, of which all citizens over eighteen were members. The Council of Five Hundred which prepared business for the Assembly and, if requested, carried out what had been decided there, was made up of citizens who were chosen by lot. The same was true of the juries. Minor officials also were chosen by lot. The chief magistrates and the highest officers in the army were elected by the Assembly. Pericles was a general, very popular, who acted for a long time as if he were head of the state, but he had to be elected every year. Freedom of speech was the right the Athenians prized most and there has never been another state as free in that respect. When toward the end of the terrible Peloponnesian War the victorious Spartans were advancing upon Athens, Aristophanes caricatured in the theatre the leading Athenian generals and showed them up as cowards, and even then as the Assembly opened, the herald asked, "Does anyone wish to speak?"

There was complete political equality. It was a government of the people, by the people, for the people. An unregenerate old aristocrat in the early fourth century, B.C. writes: "If you *must* have a democracy, Athens is the perfect example. I object to it because it is based on the welfare of the lower, not the better, classes. In Athens the people who row the vessels and do the work have the advantage. It is their prosperity that is important." All the same, making the city beautiful was important too, as were also the great performances in the theatre. If, as Plato says, the Assembly was chiefly made up of cobblers and carpenters and smiths and farmers and retail businessmen, they approved the construction of the Parthenon and the other buildings on the Acropolis, and they crowded the theatre when the great tragedies were played. Not only did all free men share in the government; the love of the beautiful and the desire to have a part in creating it were shared by the many, not by a mere chosen few. That has happened in no state except Athens.

But those free Greeks owned slaves. What kind of freedom was that? The question would have been incomprehensible to the ancient world. There had always been slaves; they were a first necessity. The way of life everywhere was based upon them. They were taken for granted; no one ever gave them a thought. The very best Greek minds, the thinkers who discovered freedom and the solar system, had never an idea that slavery was evil. It is true that the greatest thinker of them all, Plato, was made uncomfortable by it. He said that slaves were often good, trustworthy, doing more for a man than his own family would, but he did not follow his thought through. The glory of being the first one to condemn it belongs to a man of the generation before Plato, the poet Euripides. He called it, "That thing of evil," and in several of his tragedies showed its evil for all to see. A few centuries later the great Greek school of the Stoics denounced it. Greece first saw it for what it is. But the world went on in the same way. The Bible accepts it without comment. Two thousand years after the Stoics, less than a hundred years ago, the American Republic accepted it.

Athens treated her slaves well. A visitor to the city in the early fourth century, B.C., wrote: "It is illegal here to deal a slave a blow. In the street he won't step aside to let you pass. Indeed you can't tell a slave by his dress; he looks like all the rest. They can go to the theatre too. Really, Athenians have established a kind of equality between slaves and free men." They were never a possible source of danger to the state as they were in Rome. There were no terrible slave wars and uprisings in Athens. In Rome, crucifixion was called "the slave's punishment." The Athenians did not practice crucifixion, and had no so-called slave's punishment. They were not afraid of their slaves.

In Athens' great prime Athenians were free. No one told them what they must do or what they should think—no church or political party or powerful private interests or labor unions. Greek schools had no donors of endowments they must pay attention to, no government financial backing which must be made secure by acting as the government wanted. To be sure, the result was that they had to take full responsibility, but that is always the price for full freedom. The Athenians were a strong people, they could pay the price. They were a thinking people; they knew what freedom means. They knew—not that they were free because their country was free, but that their country was free because they were free.

A reflective Roman traveling in Greece in the second century A.D. said, "None ever throve under democracy save the Athenians; *they* had sane self-control and were law-abiding." He spoke truly. That is what Athenian education aimed at, to produce men who would be able to maintain a self-governed state because they were themselves self-governed, self-controlled, self-reliant. Plato speaks of "the education in excellence which makes men long to be perfect citizens, knowing both how to rule and be ruled." "We are a free democracy," Pericles said. "We do not allow absorption in our own affairs to interfere with participation in the city's; we yield to none in independence of spirit and complete self-reliance, but we regard him who holds aloof from public affairs as useless." They called the useless man a "private" citizen, *idiotes*, from which our word "idiot" comes.

They had risen to freedom and to ennoblement from what Gilbert Murray calls "effortless barbarism"; they saw it all around them; they hated its filth and fierceness; nothing effortless was among the good things they wanted. Plato said, "Hard is the good," and a poet hundreds of years before Plato said,

> Before the gates of Excellence the high
> gods have placed sweat.
> Long is the road thereto and steep and
> rough at the first,
> But when the height is won, then is
> there ease.

33

When or why the Greeks set themselves to travel on that road we do not know, but it led them away from habits and customs accepted everywhere that kept men down to barbaric filth and fierceness. It led them far. One example is enough to show the way they took. It was the custom—during how many millenniums, who can say?—for a victor to erect a trophy, a monument of his victory. In Egypt, where stone was plentiful, it would be a slab engraved with his glories. Farther east, where the sand took over, it might be a great heap of severed heads, quite permanent objects; bones last a long time. But in Greece, though a man could erect a trophy, it must be made of wood and it could never be repaired. Even as the victor set it up he would see in his mind how soon it would decay and sink into ruin, and there it must be left. The Greeks in their onward pressing along the steep and rough road had learned a great deal. They knew the victor might be the vanquished next time. There should be no permanent records of the manifestly impermanent. They had learned a great deal.

An old Greek inscription states that the aim of mankind should be "to tame the savageness of man and make gentle the life of the world." Aristotle said that the city was built first for safety, but then that men might discover the good life and lead it. So the Athenians did according to Pericles. Pericles said that Athens stood for freedom and for thought and for beauty, but in the Greek way, within limits, without exaggeration. The Athenians loved beauty, he said, but with simplicity; they did not like the extravagances of luxury. They loved the things of the mind, but they did not shrink from hardship. Thought did not cause them to hesitate, it clarified the road to action. If they had riches they did not make a show of them, and no one was ashamed of being poor if he was useful. They were free because of willing obedience to law, not only the written, but still more the unwritten, kindness and compassion and unself-ishness and the many qualities which cannot be enforced, which depend on a man's free choice, but without which men cannot live together.

If ever there is to be a truly good and great and enduring republic it must be along these lines. We need the challenge of the city that thought them out, wherein for centuries one genius after another grew up. Geniuses are not pro-duced by spending money. We need the challenge of the way the Greeks were educated. They fixed their eyes on the individual. We contemplate millions. What we have under-taken in this matter of education has dawned upon us only lately. We are trying to do what has never been attempted before, never in the history of the world—educate all the young in a nation of 170 millions; a magnificent idea, but we are beginning to realize what are the problems and what may be the results of mass production of education. So far, we do not seem appalled at the prospect of exactly the same kind of education being applied to all the school children from the Atlantic to the Pacific, but there is an un-easiness in the air, a realization that the individual is grow-ing less easy to find; an idea, perhaps, of what standardiza-tion might become when the units are not machines, but human beings.

Here is where we can go back to the Greeks with profit. The Athenians in their dangerous world needed to be a nation of independent men who could take responsibility, and they taught their children accordingly. They thought about every boy. Someday he would be a citizen of Athens, responsible for her safety and her glory, "Each one," Pericles said, "fitted to meet life's chances and changes with the utmost versatility and grace." To them education was by its very nature an individual matter. To be properly educated a boy had to be taught music; he learned to play a musical instrument. He had to learn poetry, a great deal of it, and recite it. There were a number of musical instruments and many poets; though, to be sure, Homer was the great textbook.

That kind of education is not geared to mass production. It does not produce people who instinctively go the same way. That is how Athenian children lived and learned, while our millions learn the same lessons and spend hours before television sets looking at exactly the same thing at exactly the same time. For one reason and another we are more and more ignoring differences, if not trying to obliterate them. We seem headed toward a standardization of the mind, what Goethe called "the deadly commonplace that fetters us all." That was not the Greek way.

The picture of the Age of Pericles drawn by the historian Thucydides, one of the greatest historians the world has known, is of a state made up of people who are self-reliant individuals, not echoes or copies, who want to be let alone to do their own work, but who are also closely bound together by a great aim, the commonweal, each one so in love with his country—Pericles' own words—that he wants most of all to use himself in her service. Only an ideal? Ideals have enormous power. They stamp an age. They lift life up when they are lofty; they drag down and make decadent when they are low—and then, by that strange fact, the survival of the fittest, those that are low fade away and are forgotten. The Greek ideals have had a power of persistent life for twenty-five hundred years.

Is it rational that now when the young people may have

to face problems harder than we face, is it reasonable that with the Atomic Age before them, at this time we are giving up the study of how the Greeks and Romans prevailed magnificently in a barbaric world, the study, too, of how that triumph ended, how a slackness and softness finally came over them to their ruin? In the end, more than they wanted freedom, they wanted security, a comfortable life, and they lost all—security and comfort and freedom.

Is not that a challenge to us? Is it not true that into our education have come a slackness and softness? Is hard effort prominent? The world of thought can be entered in no other way. Are we not growing slack and soft in our political life? When the Athenians finally wanted not to give to the state, but the state to give to them, when the freedom they wished most for was freedom from responsibility, then Athens ceased to be free and was never free again. Is not that a challenge?

Cicero said, "To be ignorant of the past is to remain a child." Santayana said, "A nation that does not know history is fated to repeat it." The Greeks can help us, help us as no other people can, to see how freedom is won and how it is lost. Above all, to see in clearest light what freedom is. The first nation in the world to be free sends a ringing call down through the centuries to all who would be free.

Plato put into words what that freedom is. "Freedom" he says, "is no matter of laws and constitutions; only he is free who realizes the divine order within himself, the true standard by which a man can steer and measure himself." True standards, ideals that lift up, marked the way of the Greeks. Therefore their light has never been extinguished.

"The time for extracting a lesson from history is ever at hand for them who are wise."—Demosthenes

PLATO

⚜

An Address Given Before the Classical Association of the Atlantic States

Plato is labeled a philosopher, supremely then in our eyes a theorizer—words, words, words. The notion would have horrified him. Philosophy to him was the love of wisdom, the love of seeking and finding the truth. He saw himself as a philosopher preoccupied with the most important practical truth for human beings, the good state, what it was and how it could be brought about.

When he first grew up he started his career as a practical politician and, if he could have had his desire, would always have been one. That came naturally to a young Athenian. Gilbert Murray says, "Athens was a little center of white-hot spiritual light in a world of effortless barbarism." To keep the fire blazing was a passion with each succeeding generation. Everything good for them depended on their doing so. Athens was in a poor position. She had no strong, dependable allies, and a powerful barbarian nation was perpetually threatening her. Her strength was the spirit of her citizens to whom she meant freedom and civilization, the only possibility of a good life.

38

But that was gone by the time Plato entered political life. What he came up against was political corruption, influence being bought and sold. This or that man's private gain was often the deciding motive, not the public welfare. The democracy was less than two hundred years old. The great statesmen who had brought it into being and nursed it into vigor had been men of honor and devoted patriotism and they had led a people who knew their country's good was more important to them than their own. They were a highly intelligent nation too, and yet in a few years, as history goes, they showed the world in a way it should never have forgotten how quickly honor and patriotism can cease to be the prevailing influence in a state. The Athenians' position did not change but they got used to it. Persia had not yet attacked them. Perhaps she never would. They themselves changed; instead of wanting to give to the state, they wanted the state to give to them. It was a drastic change which affected their entire lives. They had been self-reliant men, sharing in the responsibility for all. But that spirit had died down by the time Plato came. In one of his letters he writes that he saw "the written law and the customs being corrupted at an astounding rate." Socrates, the best man he knew, was put to death. It did not take Plato long to believe that he was helpless. He left politics. He left the service of the state and never entered it again and with what keen regret he shows many times. No other life could approach it in significance and importance to him. He said and always thought, "The greatest and fairest sort of wisdom by far is that which is concerned with the ordering of states." He did what he thought he could. He founded a school to train young men to be honest and wise leaders, and it became very popular although the course was very difficult. But the result was not a politically reformed Athens of honest men leading a free state. The Academy lasted for nine hundred years, but we do not know of a single notable leader who was educated there and Athens lost her freedom before it was fifty years old. The greatest alumnus who was the greatest any school anywhere ever produced, Aristotle, was interested in many things more than in politics.

But the Dialogues have come down to us, and they are enough to recompense us for Plato's failure in politics. They are unique and they are incomparable. Whether the Socrates in them is in large part a creation of Plato's or a portrait from life, we do not know. The question has been debated for hundreds of years and never settled. However that may be, the picture we are left with is extraordinarily vivid and impressive, and to the reader today it is apt to seem unimportant how much of Socrates is Plato and how much of Plato is Socrates.

The two thousand years between them and ourselves have not diminished Plato as they accumulate but rather the reverse. He belongs to the very small number who are remembered because they have had a share in establishing permanent standards for us—a matter of vital importance, but often not perceived at the time. Whenever such a one is recognized, whether Eastern or Western, Egyptian, Semite, Hindu, Chinese, European, history pauses. Plato is the mountain height of the West.

Not long ago I was talking about him with a distinguished classical professor, and he asked me which of the Dialogues meant most to me. I said I believed I read oftenest not the two generally acknowledged to be the greatest, the *Republic* and the *Symposium*, but the *Gorgias*. He smiled and

said, "About rhetoric, isn't it?" and startled me into a
fresh realization of what Plato means to me. The subject
of the *Gorgias* is rhetoric and rhetoric means nothing to
me, yet I read the *Gorgias* for my profit and delight.

The aged Gorgias, a famous teacher of rhetoric, is re-
futed by Socrates when he tries to state what is the greatest
good for mankind, and a pupil, Polus, takes up the argument for him. Polus says that the greatest good is power
and that the all-powerful tyrant is the happy man. Slowly
he is driven by Socrates to the conclusion that far from
being happy, the tyrant is more miserable than those he
injures, because to do wrong is misery; to suffer wrong is
as nothing in comparison. This statement astonishes Polus
and dismays him even while he makes it, but he sees that it
results inevitably from the argument.

At this point a third man steps in. Does Socrates think
he is turning human life upside-down? Really, he is just
talking religion. (The word used is "philosophy," but it
means what we mean by "religion.") A little religion is all
very well, even good for the young, but a man will never
gain wealth and honor that way. On the contrary, anybody
can injure him and he won't defend himself. He will let
himself be boxed on the ears with impunity! This is when
Socrates begins to talk with fervour. "We are discussing,"
he says, "who is happy and who is not, really the way human
life should be lived, and what question could be more serious."

The others state their position briefly and clearly: the
happy man is he who has let his desires grow to the utter-
most and has the power to satisfy them. Men praise self-
restraint and the like only out of weakness because they
have not the power to take what they want. Socrates re-

peats what he has said: to do wrong is the worst that can befall a man; to suffer wrong is little in comparison. His intense desire to convince his hearers grows clearer and clearer. He must induce them to see that the good is altogether different from the safe. He urges them not to mind if someone insults and strikes them. "For heaven's sake, let him, and be of good cheer." (Turn to him the other cheek also.) "You can suffer by doing right but you can never suffer harm."

The real end of the talk is the conclusion that suffering and happiness can be companions. It is the best introduction to the Sermon on the Mount that I know.

And as I read I remember what Phaedo said as he told how Socrates drank the poison in prison: "I wept—not for him, but for myself. I could not pity him. He seemed to me blessed."

Socrates was happy, not only in the sense of being blessed, of having joy—that sad word joy, as someone has said—but he enjoyed himself too, greatly. "At a festival" —the speaker is Alcibiades—"he was the only person who had real powers of enjoyment." Plato contrasts the peace of the man whose one aim is to seek and find the truth against the restlessness of the busy man who is always in a hurry because to him life is a race for success. He becomes keen and shrewd, but his soul is small and mean. Fears of risks and dangers have proved too much for his honesty and independence and growth. Yet he is sure that he knows what life is and can deal with it. Beside him the other man, who wants only the truth and who really knows, appears often very poorly, insignificant or even a failure. But if the roles are changed and the man of true wisdom draws the busy man up to contemplate what is really important, what good and evil, happiness and misery and the like really are, then the narrow keen little mind is dismayed and lost. The invisible is non-existent to him; he believes only in what he can hold in his hands. He does not know what life is, that truly to live is to strive to become like God as far as that is possible. He does not know what the certain penalty is of living as he has done—not the penalty of prison or death or anything of that sort, but the certainty that he will surely grow more and more like himself.

No writer is more anonymous than Plato. His name appears in the Dialogues only once. All the same, we can catch a glimpse of him here and there; certainly a unique individuality. What he says about the creation of the universe is a case in point.

To him the universe was intelligible, and therefore, how it came to be could be discovered by the searching intellect. In the first chapter of Genesis, "God said, 'Let there be light,' and there was light." That is not Plato's way of dealing with the matter. He thinks out how light must have come about, a marvellous contraption of myriads of triangles, and how physics began and astronomy and biology. His temper of mind nowhere even approaches the dogmatic, but in this account of the creation it is so least of all. The statements he makes are possible, he declares, even perhaps probable, but the only way to certainty about such matters would be to ask God, and that is denied us. But at the very least it is better to use one's mind on these questions than to pass them by indolently without even trying to think them out. Moreover, to do that kind of thinking is, he says, so diverting and refreshing. Plato's recipe for resting a tired mind is: "When a man relaxes and lays aside the laws of eternal being he can get innocent pleasure from contemplating the probabilities of how they came to pass and thus bring into his life a modest and reasonable entertainment."

One is left with a pleasant picture of Plato in his room in the Academy after a busy day, entertaining himself— modestly and reasonably—and resting a tired mind in his own way.

There are places too where we can see even human weakness. In one of the later dialogues, there is a striking passage about what Plato says was, "an impression of tediousness experienced in our discussion regarding the being of not-being." Here we are introduced to Plato's audience, clearly a critical one. It charged Plato with being dull, the most intolerable of all accusations because the only one nobody can defend himself against. Plato was stung by it too sharply to bear this fact in mind. His defense is made with calm superiority: "Mere length of discourse," he says, "should not offend. A length suited to give pleasure is of no importance. Brevity or length should be used as can best sharpen the wits of the hearers. A man who complains of tediousness should prove that a shorter statement would express better the truth. Any other praise or blame we should pretend not to hear." For a moment Plato stands on the ordinary human level.

A very little reading shows that there were reasons for the criticism, as for instance: "Motion is other than being and the plain result is that motion really is and is not. Then non-being necessarily exists in the case of motion, for the nature of the other makes every class other than being and we may truly say that they are not and again that they are."

"Nothing can be plainer," said a polite young man who was listening.

In a dialogue where he questions two boys, close friends, on what friendship is, there is an especially good example of his way of teaching. The boys are sure that they know, but the more they try to explain, the less they feel that they really know. They come to see under Socrates' guiding hand that every statement they make is unsatisfactory. He declares that he knows as little as they do. How ridiculous is it, he tells them at the end, that he and they who are friends should not know what friendship is.

This method is Socrates' own among the great teachers of mankind. Other teachers would have been concerned to give the boys a higher ideal of friendship, to form in their young minds a mold of nobility which might persist. Of course Socrates would have been pleased to do this too, but the reason he made no attempt was because he did not believe it could be done. It was his conviction that truth cannot be taught; it must be sought. His only desire in talking to people was to wake them up. To him the best that could be done for the boys was to arouse them to think. In that way they might finally turn their thoughts toward their own inner world and examine and learn to know themselves. "The unexamined life is not fit to be lived by a man," he said. So and only so could one discover the spark of good within, which he alone could kindle into a flame. There is no better illustration of the way Socrates taught.

When Socrates was tried and condemned to death, the *Apology*, the dialogue in which he accepted the sentence, gives a vivid picture of the man he was. Great spiritual leaders and great saints adorn the pages of history, but Socrates is not like any of them. He is, indeed, the servant of the divine power, living in complete obedience to God, yet he always views the world of men with a bit of humor, a touch of irony. He spent his life in the effort to kindle into a flame the spark of good in every man, but when he failed, when he came up against blind obstinacy or stupid conceit or the indifference of egotism, or when he drew down on himself bitter enmity, then along with his regret (because he cared for everyone) is mingled a little—not quite amusement—but a feeling, as it were, of rueful sympathy, as if he said to himself, "What silly children we are." Socrates never condemned.

Very early on the morning of the day he is to die, his devoted friend, Crito, comes to the prison to beseech him to let his friends save him. It will be easy to bribe his jailors. Crito himself has far more money than will be needed, and there are many others who are eager to contribute. Athens is not the only place where Socrates can live happily. He will find friends wherever he goes. To this Socrates answers by asking Crito if it can ever be right to defend oneself against evil by doing evil? Granted that it was unjust to condemn him to death, can it be right for him to escape by breaking the law? What will happen to a state if individuals are able to set aside the laws? A man must always do what his country orders him unless he can change her view of what the law should be. "If I leave the city I shall return evil for evil. If I die, I shall suffer, but I shall not do evil."

After his death, a pupil who had been with him to the end, Phaedo, gives an account of Socrates' last hours to a number of his friends. It was not until evening, he tells them, that Socrates drank the poison. The day had been passed in conversation, as was his way in prison or out, and the talk had turned on the immortality of the soul. Various so-called proofs were discussed, the chief one being that "our birth is but a sleep and a forgetting." In the end, however, this argument is discarded with all the others. Then Socrates brings up a new idea: the soul is immortal because it can perceive, have a share in truth, goodness, beauty, which are eternal. Man can know God because he has in him something akin to the Eternal which cannot die. This is accepted by all present.

So the long talk ends. The poison is drunk. The last words Socrates speaks show better than all the arguments what he believed about immortality. As he felt the cold of the poison creeping up to his heart he said: "Remember, I owe a cock to Aesculapius." It was the Greek custom on recovering from an illness to make an offering to the Divine Healer. To himself Socrates was not dying. He was entering not into death, but into life, "life more abundantly."

Through the centuries Plato has received his rightful tribute of deep reverence but not often of deep understanding. Indeed, he has been misunderstood to such a degree that the word "Platonic" has come to have an unreal meaning, a complete misstatement of that mighty mind. He had a great vision; he had nothing of the visionary in him. He was a very great artist; he had a supreme artist's knowledge of people, and he felt that to see them ever as finished, completed, was to stultify them. He saw them always in the presence of what he called the Beyond, never to be reached but a perpetual summons to go forward. To him the proof of Socrates' truth was his life and death. The text of the Dialogues in general might well be Christ's saying, "He that willeth to do His will shall know the doctrine whether it be of God."

One of the young men with whom Socrates had been building the Republic says to him at the end, "I do not believe such a place ever has been or ever will be." "Perhaps," Socrates answers, "a pattern of it is laid up in heaven *for him who wants to see.* But whether it exists or ever will is no matter. A man can order his life by its laws."

THE GREEK CHORUS:
FIFTEEN OR FIFTY?

When I was a girl at college I was taught a neat and simple scheme which comprised within itself all that one need know about the externals of the Greek tragic drama: three actors made up the full complement for every play; each actor was raised above the ground by means of a cothurnus or boot which had a short pillar attached to the sole; and finally the chorus always numbered fifteen. These dogmas were taught precisely as if they had come down in a book written on stage technique in the fifth century B.C. to explain to the Athenians the methods of present-day producers: Aeschylus' range as shown by the *Prometheus* and the *Oresteia*; Sophocles' greater technical skill exemplified in the rapid changes in the *Ajax*; and the details of setting and costuming by which Euripides was putting realistic drama upon the boards.

Even with such a treatise in our hands we could not have been more sure than we were that we knew the essentials of how things were done upon the stage in the golden age of Greece. To be sure, we realized that there were difficulties. The stilts, for instance, could be troublesome, as in the *Agamemnon*, when the king's boots are removed before he walks to the palace on the precious purple stuffs spread to do him honor. He would, of course, suddenly become a head shorter than the others on the stage. And if a dramatist could be allowed only three actors to carry all the characters in every play, an important role must sometimes be filled by two or even three different persons. Indeed, in the *Oedipus Coloneus* one of the parts would have to be shifted back and forth four times. As for the invariable chorus of fifteen, the only Greek play which mentions the number, the *Suppliants* of Aeschylus, refers to it always as numbering fifty.

Undoubtedly these were troubles, but they were not taken seriously. To do so would have involved looking at the plays as theatrical productions and that was never done. The scholars who established these dogmas of the Athenian stage were men of the library, not the theatre. They had deep learning and keen scholarly acumen; they tracked down every allusion in the literature of antiquity that might bear upon the matter; they deciphered old manuscripts and clarified old inscriptions. But they paid no attention to the fact that the subject of their study was, in the final analysis, a dramatic performance, and they never stopped to consider what would be the effect upon an audience of the rules and regulations they laid down so authoritatively for the tremendous living force which all great drama is.

No one else ever stopped to consider it either. Dogmas are so comfortable. One can rest in perfect peace on *ex cathedra* utterances delivered securely from the lecture platform and taken down accurately in notebooks. Both he that teaches and he that listens are soothed and sustained.

Nothing is more irritating to human nature than a perpetual question mark. The only people out of all the world who have been able to put up with it were the Athenians of the great age of Athens. The rest of us demand certainties. We have, indeed, a conviction that we—which is to say, mankind—are on our way to ultimate certainty about everything, that the path which has led us out of darkness and bewilderments of the past is conducting us toward a goal, distant indeed, but perfectly sure of attainment, where knowledge clear and full shall be grasped and held with perfect certainty.

And yet only a little reflection is necessary to show the fallacy in this pleasant reasoning. Greater knowledge and greater certainty do not by any means go hand in hand. Oftenest the very reverse is true: greater knowledge means less certainty; about a vast number of things we are certain in proportion as we do not know.

So with our dogmas of the Greek stage. Two of them have lately been re-examined in the light of wider knowledge, with the result that they have retreated from the position of certainties to that of questionable opinions. In one department, intimately concerned with the matter, we have far more knowledge than those before us had. The theatre during the last decade or two has focussed the attention of thinking people in a way it has never done before. Beyond all question we know more about it than our predecessors did; we are more keenly aware of how the drama is conditioned. People are theatre-conscious today as in no other age and, as a result, Greek tragedy has been brought out of the library on to the boards. The cothurnus and the three-actor rule have both been considered under a new aspect, their theatrical practicability. From this point of view it becomes instantly apparent that the idea of an important role being changed four times back and forth between different actors, to the entire satisfaction of the Athenian audience, is more difficult to credit than the occasional infringement of the scholars' rule of three. It is true that this conclusion does away with all the careful diagrams, as delightfully complicated as any jig-saw puzzle, which proved that three actors were factually possible, but it also restores the Athenians to the position of alert spectators, which seems no more than their due.

In the same way the old solution for those troublesome high boots of Agamemnon's—that the attendants did not pull them off, but merely pretended to do so, rested upon the assumption of a childlike naïveté on the part of the audience, who allowed the imposture and contentedly watched the king clump along on his pillars over the purple he had just declared no boot should ever touch. The cothurnus, too, has had to retreat before dramatic probability.

But so far the rule of fifteen for the chorus has not been called into serious question. The theatrical difficulty involved in it presented itself first to my mind when I was shown pictures of the performances four or five years ago of the *Prometheus* at Delphi. The tiny band of fifteen appeared ludicrously inadequate on that great orchestra surrounded by the immense auditorium with the mighty cliffs of the mountains towering above. Again it came to me with an even sharper perception when I stood in the theatre at Epidaurus, looking up to the endless tiers of seats and down to the enormous circle of the dancing floor. Fifteen performers on so vast a stage, so far removed from the spectators—and the Greeks with their sure sense for proportion in beauty. I could not bring the two ideas together. Then and there I determined to find out what was the basis for the dogma, why every writer on the subject declared that in the great age of the Athenian stage the number was fifteen.

The ancient authorities for this assertion, as mustered in the latest edition of Haigh's *Attic Theatre*, look impressive: the scholiasts on a passage in the *Birds*, the *Eumenides*, and the *Knights*; the anonymous *Life of Aeschylus*; Pollux; Photion; Tzetzes; Suidas. The array appears to the casual and even to the careful reader quite decisive. But a closer investigation brings doubts.

The scholiasts, to begin with, are far from satisfactory evidence. The title is given to the anonymous scribes whose notes are found on the margins of Greek and Latin manuscripts as explanations of some unusual word or construction or as comments upon the subject matter, and the like. Perhaps the writer himself found them on the margin of the manuscript he was copying, and some of the comments may go back to a great Alexandrian scholar's exegesis. Perhaps the writer added them to help later readers. These copyists in their turn would often change a comment to suit their own ideas as well as add others, and they continued this process on into the fifteenth century. We know nothing about these writers; we can date them only so far as we can date the manuscript in each case, and as we possess no manuscript of a Greek play older than the eleventh century, it will be seen that the manuscripts are all far removed from classical times. They can be used only with a question mark or to confirm evidence which comes from a more authoritative source.

The *Life of Aeschylus* gives the number of the chorus not as fifteen, but fourteen. One explanation for this discrepancy, that the leader of the chorus was not included, does not attempt to explain why the most important member should have been left out. The other explanation, that the scribe copied the number wrongly, is equally unsatisfactory. The scholars are, however, agreed that the part of the *Life* in which the statement about the chorus is made was written much later than the rest of the book and is far less authoritative. Unsupported, it would have little weight.

Of the four remaining witnesses, Tzetzes, who lived as late as the twelfth century, gives the number as eleven, not fifteen. He is, however, chiefly noted for his inaccuracies and his statement may be dismissed. The only matter worthy of remark in connection with him is that Haigh and Mr. Pickard-Cambridge should use his name—and, apparently, to support their own view of fifteen.

Three writers are left, upon whose authority the number fifteen mainly depends. Photion, who declares that was the number, was Patriarch of Constantinople toward the end of the ninth century, a man of wide learning and great ability, but forced by the circumstances of his life to do his writing hastily and often convicted of lack of accuracy.

Suidas, the next, cannot be exactly dated, but it is certain that he lived not earlier than the end of the tenth century. His is the famous statement that Sophocles increased the number of the chorus to fifteen from the twelve which had made up the chorus of Aeschylus, a statement accepted as authoritative by every writer on the Greek drama. The undoubted fact that Suidas has been found wrong in some of his assertions does not appear in the least to diminish the weight of his evidence on this particular point, while the great length of time that separated him from his subject, some fourteen hundred years, is never even mentioned as having a bearing on his trustworthiness. Students of the Greek drama today are taught just as authoritatively as I was that Aeschylus used a chorus of twelve and that Sophocles increased it to fifteen.

Last to be considered and most important of all is Pollux. There is never a book on the classical drama that fails to make him prominent. Indeed, he is second only to Aristotle as an authority. He was born in Egypt in the second century A.D., but he was sent to Athens as a professor by Marcus Aurelius' son, the Emperor Commodus. Ill-natured people said it was his melodious voice and not his learning that got him the post. However that may be, he was certainly a devoted student of vocabulary. It is supposed to be Pollux Lucian is attacking when he says, "If you can pick up an out-of-the-way word anywhere, you've got to drag it in, even in places that don't want it." The result of this interest was that he wrote the dictionary which has gained for him lasting fame. It is a very discursive example of its genre, containing most varied information about the words, including many quotations from authors otherwise unknown and works that have not come down to us. The passage on the Greek tragic chorus is the oldest statement we have by many centuries and deserves to be quoted in full: "Of the tragic chorus there were five lines of three and three files of five. For the chorus was fifteen. But anciently the tragic chorus was fifty, up to the *Eumenides* of Aeschylus, but in consequence of the crowd of these (i.e. the Eumenides or furies) the populace being terrified, the law contracted the chorus to the smaller number."

It will be seen at once that this statement of Pollux is in direct conflict with that of Suidas as far as Aeschylus is concerned. According to the one, Aeschylus used a chorus of fifty, according to the other, a chorus of twelve. The *Eumenides* was Aeschylus' last play. Shortly after its production in 458, he left Athens for Sicily and died there some two years later. He had no opportunity for further experimentation with the chorus. Both Pollux and Suidas cannot be right. And yet in general the writers on the subject accept both! Haigh, for example, declares Pollux to be the best authority for the chorus and then later on quotes Suidas. Only their agreement on the later number being fifteen is taken into account; their wide divergence on the earlier number is ignored.

One more support for the smaller chorus, twelve or fifteen as one chooses to look at it, is found, it is claimed, in a passage of the *Agamemnon* of Aeschylus. When the king is killed within the palace his cry is heard by the chorus who debate what is to be done. Twelve offer suggestions, each in a couplet. Suidas is proved right, then, say his followers. But just before the cry the chorus speak a single line and just after it, introducing the suggestions, a couplet which, with no harm to the sense, could be divided between two speakers. The argument for a chorus of twelve has become an argument for a chorus of fifteen. But both arguments rest upon the assumption, apparently never questioned, that every member of the chorus spoke. This is to use one assumption to prove another: there were only twelve or fifteen, therefor each spoke; each spoke, therefore there were only twelve or fifteen. But there is nothing in the text to afford any basis whatever for either assumption. If the chorus was larger, each member did not speak, and this assumption has certainly a better backing than the other, the authority of Pollux, who antedated Suidas by seven hundred years. The passage in the *Agamemnon* proves nothing and is of no importance except that it may be the reason why in the Middle Ages the number twelve became attached to Aeschylus' chorus.

This then is the foundation upon which the chorus of fifteen rests: the statement of three scholiasts and (since Tzetzes does not count and the *Life* is, in the only part which here counts, of doubtful authority) three writers of whom only one lived as near to the drama he was writing about as we do to the drama that flourished in England when Magna Charta was signed. The two others are separated from their subject by an immense span of centuries, from twelve to thirteen hundred years—years, too, which covered the period of disintegration and chaos which we call the Dark Ages. It would be extraordinary indeed if down through all that length of time the size of the fifth century chorus, the original chorus of Aeschylus, Sophocles, Euripides, had been handed on with no variation.

Something fairly certain, however, does emerge from the fact that all the so-called authorities are in substantial agreement about the number. We may feel reasonably sure that a chorus of, at any rate, not more than fifteen was used during a long enough period to make that the traditional number. But no connection can be established between this tradition and the fifth-century chorus. There is nothing, not one word anywhere, to bridge over the gap of six or seven hundred years, between that chorus and our first information about it. Such indications as there are all point to a much larger chorus.

In the day of our oldest authority, Pollux, there was a tradition of an original chorus of fifty superseded by a smaller chorus. Of course the story about the Athenians being terrified at the sight of so many furies is a fable, but back of it lies in all likelihood the fact of a drastic reduction at some time or other in the size of the chorus. This accords well, too, with the undoubted fact that the role of the chorus from the end of the fifth century on grew less and less important. There was good reason also for Pollux' number of fifty in the early chorus. Long before Aeschylus' day the Athenians had watched contests between choruses of fifty. At the great festival where the plays were produced, ten such choruses, five of men and five of boys, competed for a prize. Athens was used to the spectacle of many people moving together in the dance and to the great sound of all their voices singing in unison. She had also a large supply of citizens trained to sing and dance.

Furthermore, and quite as significant, the orchestra in the old theatre at Athens, where all the tragedies were first produced, was much larger than that in the theatre we know, which was built toward the end of the next century. It is said to have been of astonishing extent, a complete circle with a diameter of nearly eighty feet. That was the stage on which the choruses of the Periclean age performed, before audiences accustomed never to seeing less than fifty performers at a time.

The idea that to substitute for these a tiny band of twelve would find favor with such an audience could have been evolved only in the library. Any consideration of it from the point of view of the theatre shows the absurdity of it. On that great orchestra twelve little figures would be so insignificant as to seem ludicrous. One has only to imagine them on the stage of the Metropolitan Opera House to perceive their complete theatrical inadequacy, and yet that stage is notably smaller than the Athenian orchestra—ten feet shorter and more than fifteen feet less in depth. If Aeschylus did place upon the dancing floor a band totally out of proportion to it, and if the Athenians welcomed the substitution, it is the only example of malproportion exhibited and applauded during the entire course of the art of the Periclean age.

In conclusion, the way in which upholders of the small chorus dispose of the fact that in Aeschylus' *Suppliants* the number is always said to be fifty is typical of their whole attitude toward not only the chorus but the tragic drama in general. A rigid convention, say they, made it possible for fifteen to do duty for fifty. The audience was so completely imbued with the idea that a chorus must number fifteen that the absurdity of fifteen referred to as fifty passed them by. This is to ascribe to the Athenian drama in its youth conditions like those in the ages-old theatre of Mei Lan Fang. A clearly worked out pattern of human behavior, absolutely fixed and universally understood, is very slowly evolved. It had come into being on the Greek stage by the end of the second century A.D. when Pollux wrote. He tells us that an actor dressed in a certain way always represented a certain character: "The leading lady's dress is purple, with a train, and white around the lower part of the arm; the procurer wears a colored tunic and a short coat of a bright shade." Even the wig worn informed the audience what to expect: "The free old woman has white hair hanging to her shoulders. But the old woman slave has on her forehead a fillet of wool; the wholly excellent young man is beardless, dark, with thick black hair." On such a stage the number of a chorus would naturally be fixed by a rigid convention. But in the first great century of the Athenian drama there was no convention and nothing was fixed. Aeschylus created drama by introducing a second actor; a third was soon added; the role of the actor gained in importance and that of the chorus began to diminish; in Euripides' hands the realistic drama encroached upon the heroic. There was swift change in those years that saw tragedy emerge and spring straightway to heights never since surpassed. No swaddling bands of use and wont were ready at hand to hamper its free development. It was new and from its very birth a mighty force.

If then we must have a rule for the fifth century chorus, let it be of fifty, not of fifteen. But why should there be such a rule? The only possible reason for supposing that the size of the chorus was always the same is that the great orchestra demanded a large body of dancers and that the Athenians were used to fifty. But shall we then follow the procedure of the scholars in their libraries and declare that although in Euripides' *Suppliants* the chorus is stated to be seven women with their handmaidens, it must, according to our rule, have numbered fifty? Wider knowledge brings less certainty, a more open mind, an undogmatic attitude. We shall do better to acknowledge that we have no reason whatever to feel sure about the number of the early chorus. We may, however, feel sure of one thing: that men like Aeschylus, Sophocles, Euripides, always use their materials as they choose; they are never dictated to by them. If we disengage our minds from ascribing to them a rigid adherence to petty regulations, we shall find ourselves more able to understand the power that produced Greek tragedy.

COMEDY

"Comedy has been particularly unpropitious to definers," said that eminent definer, Dr. Johnson. From Aristotle, with whom everything begins, whose definition of the comical is "a certain error and turpitude unattended with pain and not destructive," to the chief moderns who have attempted the task—Meredith who calls it, "The first-born of common sense, the genius of thoughtful laughter," and Bergson who defines it as the corrective of mechanization—all who have ventured on the perilous ground seem to have justified Jean Paul Richter's airy fling at them, that the only value in the various definitions of comedy is that they are themselves comic.

There is no single formula for tears. Both tragedy and pathos may draw them forth, and no one definition can embrace these two. So also with laughter. It is on this point that the definers have come to grief. A formula that covers all the comic is of the nature of the enveloping blanket. As soon expect light and air in the folds of the one as point and illumination in the muddlement of the other. Three divisions of the comic are generally recognized: humor, wit, satire. Properly understood, there are but two; satire and irony also belong to the domain of wit. But whether the division is two- or three-fold, every all-inclusive definition fails to define. In point of fact the only illuminating definitions have come from those writers who have instinctively recognized this fact and have considered only one of the two. In these cases it is always wit that is considered and humor disregarded. The reason is that wit, being of the mind alone, has the clarity and sharp outline that tempts to definition, while humor is of the heart as well as of the head, a combination hard on those that love the pigeon-hole. The union of mind and heart has ever produced stumbling blocks to the definer. Religion and poetry are their products as well as humor, and the pursuer of the definition is wise to turn aside from them.

If this two-fold division is accepted, wit covering the purely intellectual side and humor that which is emotional as well, it is apparent that under the latter must be placed all that we understand by slapstick and the like. These are clearly not of the mind. The point, however, is immaterial in a consideration of the comic in literature where the question is considerably limited and the discussion of it facilitated. What causes a laugh when a fat man falls, what makes the new-born baby smile, and all like matters, so delightful to the psychological searcher into the comic, can be completely dismissed by the critic. The divisions in the drama are clear cut: there is comedy, which is either comedy of wit or of humor, and there is farce, so-called comedy of situation, which belongs in another category and is comedy only by courtesy. The fun of farce is neither of the mind nor of the heart; it is the fun of circumstance. Comedy is concerned only with human beings, "the way they are, the way they talk, the way they walk;" everything not human is alien to it. Farce is concerned only with what happens to people; it might be called the comedy of events. Such divisions as Romantic Comedy, Learned Comedy, Comedy of Intrigue, and the like, are not based upon distinctions in the nature of the comic. Romance is not comic. A romantic play with comic scenes is a comedy only so far as these predominate, and in so far as it is a comedy it belongs to the division of wit or of humor.

Poetic Comedy can also be dismissed. Poetry and comedy have no meeting ground. It is true that there is in Shakespeare a kind of poetry which is frequently confused with humor and is remotely allied to it. Jacques often gives it utterance, as when he meets the fool who says:

> . . . very wisely, "It is ten o'clock:
> Thus we may see," quoth he, "how the world wags:
> 'Tis but an hour ago, since it was nine;
> And after one hour more, 'twill be eleven;
> And so, from hour to hour, we ripe and ripe,
> And then, from hour to hour, we rot and rot,
> And thereby hangs a tale."

The familiar "all the world's a stage" will occur at once as an instance. This poetry is near to humor, and yet it is not humor. It is whimsical; it arouses not laughter but thought. The spirit of fun is so far from it that it is, above all, pensive. It is poetry, not comedy.

The same thing may be said of another kind of poetry also often met with in Shakespeare. Mercutio's speech is an example:

> O! then I seen Queen Mab hath been with you.
> She is the fairies' midwife, and she comes . . .
> Drawn with a team of little atomies

Athwart men's noses as they lie asleep.
Her wagon spokes made of long spinners' legs;
The cover, of the wings of grasshoppers;
Her traces, of the smallest spider's web.
And in this state she gallops night by night
Through lovers' brains and then they dream of love—

This poetry of the fairy tale has a delicate delightfulness which must bring a smile, but there is nothing in it that approaches the comic. It springs from neither mind nor heart but purely from the fancy. Laughter is too robust for it. It is "so thin of substance as the air"—a poet's dream. There is no poetry that is comic. Molière is called by common consent a great comic poet, but he has nothing of the poet in him unless the word is used to cover all creative genius. The entire range of his comedy of wit, irony, and satire is by its very nature unpoetical. It is the creation of the crystal-clear intellect, at the farthest remove from that which allies the lunatic, the lover, and the poet. If Aristophanes is a poet, it is only in the lyrical parts of his plays; there is nothing that could conceivably be construed as poetry in the humorous parts. Shakespeare's comedy is written in prose, not blank verse. It must be so. Comedy has to do with the surface of life. Beneath the surface there is that which is not comic, and poetry's concern is only with the reality that lies beneath. Comic poetry is a contradiction in terms. When comedy enters, poetry departs.

Molière once said that it was more difficult to write comedy than tragedy, and he added wistfully: "C'est une étrange entreprise que celle de faire rire les honnêtes gens." He meant he could have made them weep more easily; sentiment was in his mind, not the heights of tragic exaltation where only poets walk. If he had said that great com-

edy is rarer than tragedy, the facts would bear him out. It is
not to be supposed that it is harder to make people laugh
than to lift and exalt them, but it is a fact that many more
great dramatists have turned to tragedy than to comedy.
To run through the list is to become aware that geography
has played a part in the matter. The Comic Muse has her
favorites among the peoples of the earth; she prefers the
south of Europe to the north. In Italy the Commedia
dell'Arte testifies to her presence; Spain has her own comedy of breathless adventure with tragedy hovering near;
France with Molière is pre-eminent. But in the north,
laughter comes less easily. There are giants of the stage
there; Ibsen, Strindberg, Schiller. There is Goethe, a very
god. But these have no commerce with comedy. The north-
ern playwrights, it would seem, see life austerely, a land-
scape snow covered, wind swept. Gleams of comedy are
very few; the most notable is the Danish Holberg. Lessing,
the chief German, has been placed forever by Meredith's
wit: "he tried his hand at comedy with a sobering effect
on spectators." Russian comedy is negligible save for one
name, Gogol. The list, it will be seen, is very small. England remains, but if Shakespeare is as always the *exceptum
excipiendum*, her best comedy writers have not been of the
undiluted British stock, but rather of John Bull's Other Is-
land. Of the Restoration dramatists one was Irish, another
was brought up in Ireland, all five had lived long in France.
Goldsmith was Irish; Sheridan, too. So were Wilde and
Bernard Shaw. The self-conscious Nordic does not seem
congenial to the Muse of Comedy, but the reason lies in
the fact that wit is of the south chiefly, and humor of the
north, and that literary comedy is pre-eminently comedy
of wit.

The comedy of wit derives from one man who has dominated the stage for well on to three hundred years, the supreme master, the embodied genius, of thoughtful laughter, Molière. He has dominated not only the stage but the very idea of the comic. Read any definition of it: ten to one you are reading a definition of Molière. Bergson says: "The comic arises when a group, silencing emotion and calling only intelligence into play, concentrate upon one of their number." This is not a description that applies to the birth of Pantagruel, or to Falstaff's paternal lecture to the prince, or to Don Quixote and the wind mills; it is an exact description of *Le Tartuffe*, *Le Misanthrope*, *L'Avare*. Goldoni holds that the underlying idea of the comic is to correct faults and foibles; Diderot says: "Gay comedy's purpose is to ridicule and chastise vice;" Hazlitt's statement is that the comic genius takes the mask from ignorance and conceit; Meredith declares that it springs "to vindicate reason, common sense, rightness and justice; for no vain purpose ever;" Bernard Shaw says that it exists "for the correcting of pretentiousness, of inflation, of dullness." All are descriptions in brief of Molière.

A Molière comedy has for its avowed purpose instruction in the moralities. It is a sermon, not always in disguise. Vices, weaknesses, faults, are held up to ridicule. The world of his stage is the world of society, and he is forever showing up the inconsistencies and absurdities and hypocrisies of the social scheme. Seriousness is always very near. It is satire, gentle satire for the most part, sometimes bitter satire. This description clearly fits the modern makers of the English drama of ideas quite as well as it does Molière. It might stand without the alteration of a word for Shaw, Galsworthy, Granville Barker. Wilde's comedy is essentially of the genre. English Restoration comedy is Molière as the court of Charles II understood him. Goldsmith and Sheridan are his followers. It needs not to be pointed out that he created French comedy. He set the model to which all French playwrights turn. The fact is recognized and requires no buttressing, but he did the same thing for the stage of the civilized world. All comedy everywhere since Molière harks back to him, in Russia as in Spain, in Italy as in Germany. Benavente is Molière's descendant, not Calderón's; Gogol's *Revizor* is built on his model; Goldoni used to say when he saw a new play of his on the stage, "It is good but it is not yet Molière;" Lessing avowedly took him as his master. Had ever any genius such a following? He made the world forget that any other kind of comedy was possible.

In what does the peculiar greatness of Molière's comedy consist? To describe the superlatively excellent in superlatives is easy, but how describe it when all superlatives, all glowing language, must be rejected as not consonant with the subject? There are no sweeping flights in Molière, no purple passages. He is the lover of the golden mean; he is common sense incarnate. *Goût et mesure,* so valued by his countrymen, are his beyond any other writer. He is the exemplification of nothing in excess, a Greek in his art of omission. He is not quite the laughing philosopher but perfectly the smiling philosopher; he looks at life with detachment. His comedy is elegant comedy, brilliant comedy. There are no undertones "where more is meant than meets the ear." All is clarity, the clear light of keen, calm reason. Each of his great characters is at once an individual and a type, a supreme achievement. Tartuffe is an individual, a big fat man with a very red mouth and a soft cush-

iony tread and a trick of persuasive speech; a *bon viveur*
and a sensualist; he is also not a hypocrite but *the* hypocrite. His maker has not only depicted his hypocrisy with
such complete fidelity that the vice is stamped clearly forever more, but he has at the same time so heightened it—
l'exagération juste is the French phrase—that hypocrisy is
embodied in Tartuffe. He is more a type than an individual; his truth is that universal truth which Aristotle said
was truer than the particular, individual truth of history.
He is a great artistic creation; he is not a living human
being. Like all of Molière's characters he moves on the
stage, not in real life. Always, above all, Molière is a master
of the stage. Take M. Jourdain, for instance, receiving his
dancing master in night cap and dressing gown, displaying
proudly the magnificent waistcoat and "shorts" underneath,
and when the dancing master insists that a gentleman must
carry a hat in a minuet, not understanding and putting it
on top of the night cap, and so dancing the stately measure.
The comedy, as so often in Molière, is directed to the eye,
not the ear. It is masterly stagecraft. We are used to it by
now. Every comedy we see depends on it. But Molière
created it. The comedy of wit at its perfection is then a
moral pointed by delicate satire against a social vice embodied in a clearly depicted individual set off by brilliant
talk and by a consummate stage technique.

"Laughter," said Lord Chesterfield, "is illiberal and
bred. He was voicing the Molière tradition. The comedy
wit had taken possession of the stage and the days of rol-
licking, irresponsible fun were gone. In the two supreme
ages of the drama, Elizabethan England and the Athens
of Pericles, the step from the sublime to the ridiculous had
been easily taken. Uproarious comedy had flourished side

by side with gorgeous tragedy, and when one passed away the other passed away too. There is a connection between the sublime and the ridiculous. The comedy of humor, which is Aristophanes' comedy and, pre-eminently, Shakespeare's comedy—and theirs alone—has a kinship with tragedy. "The drama's laws the patrons give." The audiences to whose capacity for heightened emotion *Lear* and the *Oedipus Rex* were addressed were the same that delighted in Falstaff and in Aristophanes' maddest nonsense, and when an age succeeded in no wise less keen intellectually but of thinner emotions, great comedy as well as great tragedy departed. Aristophanes had no followers. Shakespeare stands completely isolated. His descendants are not on the stage. They are to be found in the great English humorists, and also in the writers of that delightful, unmitigated nonsense which is the bewilderment of the foreigner and understood only by the Anglo-Saxon mind. *Alice in Wonderland* came from one of Shakespeare's family. But their medium has never been the drama. The two supreme geniuses of the comic stage have had a singularly different fate: no comedy has ever been modelled upon Shakespeare; all comedies have been modelled upon Molière. The comedy of wit has dominated the comedy of humor.

The reason for this—numerical—supremacy is to be found in the nature of the comedy of humor, that is, in Shakespeare's comedy. This is not to say that all his comedy is humorous, but his great comedy, his own comedy, is comedy of humor. Almost any one of Falstaff's speeches could be given as an example. In the second act of *Henry IV*, Part One, he assumes the part of the king and reads the prince a paternal lecture:

FALSTAFF: Harry, I do not only marvel where thou spendest thy time, but also how thou art accompanied. . . . There is a thing, Harry, which thou hast often heard of, and it is known to many in our land by the name of pitch. This pitch, as ancient writers do report, doth defile; so doth the company thou keepest . . . And yet there is a virtuous man whom I have oft noted in thy company, but I know not his name.

PRINCE HENRY: What manner of man, an it like your majesty?

FALSTAFF: A goodly portly man, i' faith, and a corpulent; of a cheerful look, a pleasing eye, and a most noble carriage; and, as I think, his age is fifty, or by'r Lady, inclining to three score, and now I remember me, his name is Falstaff.

That this is high comedy no one would deny, but it teaches no lesson, it points no moral. Has it a purpose at all? Only, it would seem, to amuse. It is gay, irresponsible fun. No brilliancy of wit is there, and never a hint of satire, only laughter, the laughter of those who love what they laugh at.

In A *Midsummer Night's Dream*, Bottom would act every part in the play:

BOTTOM: Let me play the lion too: I will roar, that I will do any man's heart good to hear me; I will roar that I will make the Duke say, "Let him roar again, let him roar again."

QUINCE: An you should do it too terribly, you would fright the Duchess and the ladies, that they would shriek; and that were enough to hang us all.

ALL: That would hang us, every mother's son.

BOTTOM: I grant you, friends, if you should fright the ladies out of their wits, they would have no more discretion but to hang us; but I will aggravate my voice so, that I will roar you as gently as any sucking dove; I will roar you an 'twere any nightingale.

There could be nothing more comic than this, but the laughter it evokes is not thoughtful laughter; there is not a trace of "mechanical, automatic inelasticity contrasted with human flexibility"; it is not directed against any social vice. It has no place in any of the categories of the comic. It is just enchanting nonsense; nothing more—and nothing less—than super-excellent fooling.

Are we so made that we cannot place great value upon pure fun unless we find some trace of high truth in it? To the earnest minded this may be said in its behalf: pure fun frees us for a precious moment from our tiresome selves. Great tragedy, great music, the world of out-of-doors, have also this freeing power but not a whit more than whole-hearted laughter. Touch it with the least bit of derision— wit, irony or satire—and we are self-conscious again, but unalloyed fun that never looks before or after is of those who open the prison doors.

The *Merry Wives* has all the matter for a Molière play. The virtue of two honest married women tempted by Falstaff, the embodiment of sensual lust, the plot that foils him and reveals his villainy—it is a perfect setting for a comedy of thoughtful laughter. Molière would have treated it after the manner of the golden mean, holding the just balance between seriousness and gaiety until the end, when the lustful knight would have been shown in all the loathliness of sensual vice and punished with whips of scorpions. Thereafter Falstaff would be a synonym for fleshly vileness. None of all that moral earnestness so much as touches this comedy of humor. Not only we ourselves but the people of the play laugh very kindly at the wicked fat man. His evil designs are foiled, of course; he is shown up in the end to all; but the only result is an invitation to him to sup a posset with them and laugh at those that nor are laughing at him. It has just been a sport, says Mistress Page, fit for a laugh around a country fire. There stands Sir John, very crest-fallen but with a twinkle in his eye, and the spectator's heart goes out to him in his deserved affliction. The comedy of humor never sits in the seat of judgment; it never condemns. Judgment is for the disinterested spectator, and philosophic detachment is not more alien to the poet than to the humorist.

Bergson, writing again with Molière in his mind, says that tragedy is concerned with individuals and comedy with classes. Shakespeare is not concerned with classes or with types. His characters are individuals, people in real life, and we never think of them as personages of the stage. Falstaff sits at his ease in his inn; he walks the London streets; it is always the background of life he moves against; it is inconceivable that he should be placed forever on the theatre boards. Is it a stage wood and moonlight of the electric arc that comes to mind with Bottom and his crew? The green plot is their stage, the hawthorn their tiring-house, the chaste beams of the wat'ry moon their light. To think of Beatrice and Benedict is to be transported to an orchard as inevitably as to think of Alceste and Célimène is to be in fancy seated before the footlights.

Set thus side by side, it can be seen why the comedy of

wit has been favored to the exclusion of the comedy of humor. Wit is born of thought; humor is spontaneous. A formula for the comedy of wit is possible; a recipe can be made out of it. But as well try to imprison poetry in a formula as humor. The type, the class, can be generalized, but no formula for the individual has ever been discovered.

Life is the keynote to the comedy of humor. Its aim is not to clarify the mind and help it to knowledge—that is for the comedy of wit. It helps us to understand. *Tout comprendre, c'est tout pardonner.* It seeks not more light but more life. The comedy of wit is the white light of the unbiased intellect turned upon human follies. The comedy of humor is the laughter of "the mighty master of the human heart." The comedy of wit is true to art; the comedy of humor is true to life.

TRAGEDY
AS THEY ORDER IT
IN FRANCE

"Sublime without ever losing elegance." So say the French of Corneille and Racine, to Frenchmen the two mountain-peaks of their literature. The combination is arresting. We should find it difficult to parallel in English literature. In truth we do not want a parallel. Sublimity and elegance do not seem to us to go well together; we like them better apart, or, rather, we do not really like elegance anywhere. It suggests to us not art, but artificiality. Even worse, it has become insipid.

But it is quite otherwise in France. What they consider their greatest century is especially distinguished for elegance, the incomparable elegance which obtained amid the courtly, patterned splendor of Louis XIV, when good breeding was lord of all—dignity, self-restraint, the instinct for propriety, a quick delicacy of feeling, the avoidance of everything not agreeable. Just as at Versailles from palace and park was shut out any suggestion of the rudeness and crudeness on the other side of the walls, so from the literature of the age everything was shut out that bore any resemblance to rude and crude life as it was actually lived.

Racine, the story goes, one evening was summoned to read the Roi Soleil to sleep. A volume of Plutarch was in his hand when he appeared and the king objected. So outspoken an author could never soothe him, but only irritate his sensibilities. Ah, but, the poet told him, he would not read him *au naturel*, but so polish and omit that not one word would be left which could even surprise, much less offend, the royal ears. If only we had an account of those emendations of the gentle and urbane Plutarch, we should have a lively realization of the elegance standardized at Versailles.

French tragedy lived up to the standard. Sublimity was presented with perfect elegance.

Corneille was born soon after Henry of Navarre had ended the terrible "Wars of Religion," and well on to a hundred years after the vivid young life of the French Renaissance had shriveled up under their fierce fanaticism. France was sick to death of massacres and martyrdoms, all set to welcome a king who thought a Mass a small price to pay for Paris—"*Paris vaut bien une messe.*" What could be better fitted to extinguish the fire of hatred, the deadly *odium theologicum*, than Henry's jesting cynicism. The king who joked about the Mass—who was neither Catholic nor Protestant—the country took to its heart and with deepest relief saw, instead of bloody-minded theologies, the establishment of law, instead of confusion, "order, heavenly nurse of all the muses."

A time comes in every distracted country when order seems preferable to all else, far and away to be prized beyond liberty, and that time had come in France when

Henry began, and the two almighty cardinal rulers carried on and Louis XIV completed, the reign of law in matters small and great, the codification of the right rules for giving pleasure as well as for paying taxes. *Il faut plaire, mais selon les règles.* The Académie was born to teach correctness to genius, and the young Corneille, impelled to be a playwright, sat himself down first and drew up a set of Rules to be Followed in Writing Tragedy.

It was an action carefully to be noted by those who would understand the French genius. In Corneille's idea that the clear formulation of the rules must precede the writing of the poem lies the fundamental difference between the tragedy of France and that of all other countries.

He had no thought that his task would be made easier thereby, nor any wish, either. The easy way out, slovenly thinking, loose, slip-shod verse, prose which puts upon the reader the exertion of discovering the meaning, is not the French way out.

> *Oui, l'oeuvre sort plus belle*
> *D'une forme au travail*
> *Rebelle . . .*

Corneille would have understood that verse through and through. His rules were often exceedingly troublesome— the unities, for instance. How keep within a single four-and-twenty hours a play in which a pagan, barely turned Christian and passionately in love, becomes enamored of martyrdom, rejects his love, and dies a martyr's death? How confine to one place an action which shifts continually between an emperor and men conspiring to kill him? The imperial throne-room is an unchancy spot for conspirators. The keen-minded young man bent upon making masterpieces *selon les règles*, was perfectly aware of these difficulties, but it never occurred to him to dispense with the unities in favor of the probabilities.

He had no desire to be free to follow his impulses. He wanted to submit his genius to discipline and to wrestle with the unities. A drama which could wander from England to France and back again, or which could begin with a heroine's birth and end with her betrothal, would have seemed to him without form and void, not matter for the exigencies of art.

It is true that he sometimes found it impossible to attain the impeccable correctness of his ideal. "In *Le Cid*," he says regretfully, "the rule of twenty-four hours hurries overmuch the action," but the fault is his, not the rule's. "Also in this drama," he continues, "the unity of place has been only imperfectly maintained," but he begs the audience's leniency on this point for the reason that "if the father, waiting for his son, were to utter his lamentations in the street, a crowd would certainly gather. He must utter them in a house." Still, Corneille feels the lapse too serious to be thus passed over. If such latitude seems undesirable, "then," he says, "let him lament in the street and suppose by a fiction of the theatre that a crowd does not gather." But never do his difficulties lead him even to suggest that there might be something wrong with the unities.

He saw in them a guide to that fair, ordered clarity which was not only imposed upon him by the spirit of the age, but was a necessity of his own nature. No divided, wavering interests, but a single action which should motivate every word spoken. No different *mises-en-scène* to distract the attention, but one setting alone which could be dismissed from the mind as soon as seen. No long-past events to burden the memory, but only the immediate, visible present. So would the spectators be set free to concentrate on the essential. The unities agreed well with clarity.

Goethe once said to Eckermann that to English writers reflection was nothing, inspiration everything. There is truth in the statement. We like to think of Shakespeare carelessly throwing off his masterpieces under the compulsion of his genius. We do not think of him as analyzing methods to produce desired effects. It would not please us to imagine him pacing the floor for hours on end to find the one, the flawless, word. Inspiration, we feel, does not need all that carefulness. Daniel Webster, asked how he had been able on the spur of the moment to deliver a speech which annihilated his opponent, answered that it was perfectly easy: "I stood up and a smoking thunderbolt came by and I seized it and hurled it at him." The thunderbolt is a good image of our idea of inspiration, a power unfettered by any orderly procedure, in no way *selon les règles*. From Greek days on, it has been likened to madness. Socrates declares that, "he, who not being inspired and having no touch of madness in his soul, thinks that he will get into the temple by the help of art—he, I say, and his poetry are not admitted."

It is a far cry from that idea to the young Frenchman drawing up his rules. As Corneille saw the matter, madness and beautiful technique did not go together, and equally important with grandeur of conception was polished perfection of execution. Sublimity certainly, but elegance no less.

The point must not be obscured by our notion—and disdain—of elegance. French elegance has nothing to do with ornamentation or with anything superfluous. It is dependent upon lucidity, that crystalline lucidity which France loves above all else. Lucidity must clear the ground for elegance which cannot exist in the presence of disorder or bewilderment or mystery. The brooding forest must give way to the park open to the sunlight and everywhere exquisitely ordered. So a great modern French critic speaks of "the haphazard of inspiration" as contrasted with "the gift of fine craftsmanship." Seventeenth-century France was in love with the beauty of finished craftsmanship and did not want the least touch of madness.

It seems a strange stage for tragic poetry. To us the atmosphere of a tragedy is heavy with impending evil and dark forebodings. The scenery too, the storm-swept moor in *Lear*, Macbeth's castle where it is always night, haunted Elsinore. But the setting of a French tragedy is always brightly familiar, a room, any room, a street, the epitome of all streets. There is nothing in the play to be helped by scenery, nothing veiled or left half suggested, no hint of something inexpressible. On the contrary, the power of definite and complete expression is the very heart of Corneille's drama. He is not only able to put adequately into words all that he has in mind, he depends almost wholly on words for his interest. There is practically no action in his plays. What the actors do is to talk, or, rather, to argue with each other. It is excellent argument if Corneille's premises are granted, admirably logical, sharp-cut, maintaining an astonishing degree of intensity. Although the situation is usually improbable in the extreme and the point of view almost incredible, the dialogue is so good that all else is oftener than not lost sight of. The hero's point is so well taken, it seems impossible that the heroine can find anything to answer, but she does and with such wit, one thinks there is nothing he can oppose to it. But again he counters with something ingenious and surprising, and so it goes on, a keen debate which never slips up, but keeps one perpetually wondering what can be coming next and sometimes rises to excitement.

Throughout the characters show a perfect high breeding. No matter how crucial the stake, even if life or death hangs upon the issue of the argument, the courtesy required of antagonists on the dueling field marks these fencers with words. In *Théodore*, when a hostile stepmother declares that since her stepson is so modest in his claims, she intends to make the facts correspond to his feelings, his answer to the veiled threat is, "You can take nothing from me since I owe you all. He who owns only what he owes cannot lose." And when she goes on to enumerate all she has done for him, his sole retort is to remind her that the one way to have a favor gratefully remembered is for the donor to forget it. They all have beautiful manners. Médée, freeing the king of Athens from the prison where Jason has thrown him, asks him to give her a place of refuge from her enemies, to which he answers: "The honor of receiving one who is herself so great a hostess will efface the sadness of my misfortunes here. Dispose, Madame, of my country, which henceforth will live beneath your laws." Nicomède, when he returns in triumph from his conquests, tells the king, "My only ambition is to be able to lay another crown at your feet and to thank you for having had the goodness to make use of me." Caesar and Cleopatra vie with each other in stately compliments. Caesar assures her that if there is a man more worthy of her than he, he will resign all rights to her save one alone, that of being forever her servant, while she tells him that in showing his greatness he shows her also her own unworthiness.

This is the theatre of aristocracy. Never a bourgeois steps upon the stage. The characters move in state, heads high, eyes aloof, not disdainful of lower levels, merely unaware of them. Modern dress for them could not enter the most audacious mind. They were conceived in the grand century and they will forever stay there.

All this is again curiously unlike our idea of a tragedy. It agrees perfectly with the comedy of manners of its most elegant, the drama at the farthest remove from the heights where Aeschylus walked, and Shakespeare, when he chose. And yet to the French, lofty grandeur is Corneille's distinguishing characteristic. He is sublime above all other writers, above Racine even. What is this French sublime? It does not seek to arouse pity and terror. The heroes and heroines of these plays are so superior to both emotions, it is impossible for the spectator to feel them. It is as if he would disgrace creatures that move at such an elevation by admitting pity for them, and how feel fear in the presence of those whose most ardent desire is for a glorious death? These personages have no weaknesses. There is not the slightest attempt to present them as human beings, and the world they inhabit is as unreal as themselves.

In *Le Cid*, Corneille's best-known play if not his masterpiece, the Cid and Chimène love each other with a burning passion, but the Cid's father, a feeble old man, receives a blow from Chimène's father, and as he has not the strength to return it, becomes on the moment a man dishonored in the eyes of all. His son's duty is clear: at whatever cost to his heart he must challenge and kill Chimène's father, and so he does. Chimène's duty is equally clear. Although she cannot defend her father's act she must avenge him by bringing about her lover's death. He comes to tell her that he wants only to die; she tells him that she knows he did his duty in taking her father's life, but that her duty to take his is no less sacred. "You showed yourself worthy of me by doing me this wrong, and I by your death must show myself worthy of you."

After he leaves her, however, the Cid gloriously repulses an attack of the Moors against the town—one of the occasions when the unities are hard upon the poet—with the result that when Chimène appears at court to demand his death as the slayer of her father, the king, the only person in the play occasionally visited by other considerations than the demands of "la gloire," tells her that if he kills the Cid, the Moors will certainly kill all of them. Chimène to whom, of course, this prospect means nothing at all, declares that she will then give her hand and her fortune to whoever brings her her lover's head, and one of the courtiers engages to do so.

In the next scene the Cid presents himself before Chimène and tells her he has dared to come only because he is about to die and must bid her farewell. Die! she cries. At the hands of a weakling like that. Are you become a coward? What! he cries in his turn. Does she think he will defend himself against her champion? Of course, the man who fights for her will find in him a willing victim. "Enraptured at the thought that his blows really come from you, I will open my bosom to them, adoring in his hand your own." This bothers Chimène. She does not want the Cid to die. But how counter his point of honor with one still more pointed? To the reader it seems impossible, but Corneille is never at a loss. Will he take away her father's honor after taking away his life, she asks? How not, if he who conquered her father allows himself to be conquered by one so inferior? The way the Cid in his turn counters this, and the final result of all these points and counterpoints must be left to the curious reader. Enough has been said to show the lofty plane on which the drama moves.

It is the plane common to all of Corneille's tragedies. His heroes and heroines, to quote his own words, "regard their misfortunes with so disdainful an eye that never could they wring one word of lament from them." In *La Mort de Pompée*, the hero, stabbed by a traitor, dying "recalls only the glory of his life and holds the treachery too much beneath him to give it a thought." His wife, hating Caesar as the cause of his death, nevertheless tells him of a conspiracy of the Egyptians to kill him, but when he thanks her, she assures him that she thirsts for his ruin, only, however, in fair and open enmity, by an honorable hand animated by herself. "Thus I would sacrifice you worthily and nobly to Pompey's spirit." When Cinna tells his ladylove that no matter what happens to him, he will joyfully try to kill Augustus because he is doing it for her, she answers that success or failure should mean the same to him, since they will be equally glorious. Only his life, she reminds him, is in peril, not his honor. "Love you!" cries Aristie to Sertorius. "Sighs and raptures are for small souls. We have kingdoms to protect."

Yet love, too, soars to empyrean heights. In *Polyeucte*, Pauline's rejected lover declares that all his martial exploits had but one object, "to seek a death worthy of the man who loved her." Says Persée to Andromède, "If my death will free you from even a little trouble I shall die without regret," "Et mon trépas n'aura que d'aimables moments/

S'il vous ôte un obstacle à vos contentements." Perhaps the highest height of all is reached by Don Sanche d'Aragon, who mistakenly believing himself of low birth and forced by the queen to declare his love for her, tells her, nevertheless, that if she could so forget herself as to be touched by his base-born passion, if he were to see her descend to him from her throne, then "ceasing to honor you, I would cease to love you."

This is the French sublime, the portrait of a being—one cannot say human being—so immeasurably lifted above weaknesses as to think death the merest trifle, so completely untouched by misfortunes as hardly to be aware of them. This heroic elevation constitutes Corneille's sublimity in the eyes of his countrymen. The great French critics repeat the same idea in much the same words. They tell us, "Corneille elevated both the French language and the French soul;" "His drama has produced upon us the greatest impression of human grandeur men have ever known;" "How I adore him, master of honor and loyalty, who lifts me to his heights;" "We watch his passionate and extraordinary souls and we feel that we are masters of our fate;" "France found in him the laws of the grandeur of the soul" (*les règles* again). They write about him as Fundamentalists do about the Bible: "He lifts us above ourselves to a state of moral exaltation;" "He has taught us the heroism of duty, the beauty of sacrifice;" "He is the poet of loftiness of soul to whom the highest beauty is the beauty of holiness."

It is a conception of tragic sublimity which belongs to France alone. Greek and English tragedy do present beings greater of stature than mere man, but human, even so, and pitiable exceedingly, unable for all their magnificence to surmount man's lot, to suffer wrong and anguish and to die. Watching them we pity all mankind—"man, created sick, commanded to be whole." But Corneille's heroes are armored against life's ills, wrapped in their own loftiness. There is never a sense of fellow-feeling in following them. We are interested in them for the reason that they are true to their extraordinary selves, but it is the interest of curiosity, not sympathy.

Here is the clue to French tragedy. Its aim is not to set the hearer to weeping or to trembling, but to arouse his attention to the pure grandeur of the heroic. When Mme. de Sévigné "yielded six reluctant tears" to Racine's *Andromaque*, she was moved to the utmost that Corneille too would have desired. The way to elevate his audience to tragic heights, as he saw that *étrange entreprise*, was not to plunge them into a welter of the emotions, but to lift them above themselves by the contemplation of transcendent greatness. He summoned them to admire, and admiration is of the head and not the heart.

This is the dividing line between French tragedy and the tragedy of Shakespeare and the Greeks. To Corneille the intelligence held first place. His sharp-pointed dialogue that culminated always in some expression of lofty disinterestedness was directed to quicken the mind, to kindle the spirit to appreciate the grand and the noble, not to soften the heart. For all the romantic extravagance of his plots, he was primarily an intellectual. In view of the way the Cid and Chimène are actuated, it is perhaps as well to remind the reader at this point that the intellectual and the rational are by no means the same, as witness all the mediaeval scholars who exercised their undoubted intellects on the angels and the needle's point. They were doing only what the intellect always must do: they were trying to clarify and simplify. They would not put up with vague notions about the amount of space a nonspatial being occupied, but proceed by due process of logic to determine exactly how many the needle's point could accommodate.

In the same way Corneille set out to clarify and simplify tragedy. He did not put his mind upon his premises any more than the scholars did, but, like them, he would have nothing to do with the vague or the illogical, no dealings whatsoever with the unintelligible, whether in fate or in human beings. He turned away with complete finality from that which baffles us in Aeschylus or in Shakespeare, that which "forces us to reflect and yet find our reflection fail us," Cordelia's death or Hamlet's or Cassandra's. Polyeucte dies a triumphant martyr, who has preferred the eternal joys of heaven to the brief joys of earth, who has, in other words, made an intelligent choice and is perfectly aware that he has done so. There is a reason in things, Corneille tells us. The hero justifies pain. An unjust death, as all unjust suffering, can be glorious and therefore well for him who suffers and those whom he fires to admiration. But Lear with the dead Cordelia in his arms stands where the reason is abashed and admiration not so much as dreamed of.

To propound a problem thus and leave it unsolved would have been to Corneille bad art—merely to lift the curtain for "a glimpse of incomprehensibles and Thoughts of things which Thoughts do but tenderly touch." The very idea of such a vague illimitable "beyond the last peaks and all seas of the world" would have tried him sorely. Art was something else—balance, rhythm, symmetry, above all, clarity. Not the towering mountain veiled in mist, but the stone hewn to the sharp-cut line.

The poet's task was not merely to suggest. That would be to refuse to carry the burden himself and to shift it to others. He must find expression for everything he had in mind, fully and also simply and lucidly.

> If all the pens that poets ever held
> Had fed the feeling of their master's thoughts—
> If these had made one poem's period,
> And all combined in beauty's worthiness,
> Yet should there hover in their restless heads
> One thought, one grace, one wonder, at the least,
> Which into words no virtue can distil.

Corneille would never have agreed. Undoubtedly he would have considered Marlowe's idea an easy excuse for faulty workmanship. His verses, those rolling Alexandrines, which give such an intensity of pleasure to the French ear and produce even upon the foreigner an impression of power, of majesty, are of all the poetry of the post-Greek world the most direct, the least adorned, singularly devoid of poetry's stock-in-trade: of adjectives few; of metaphors, similes, figures of speech, fewer.

It is not for the foreigner to select at his own preference examples to show Corneille's greatness as a poet, but more than one French critic has quoted as illustrating to perfection the splendid sweep of Corneille's verse, together with his direct simplicity of statement, a passage from *Attila* where Ildione tells the man she loves why she is going to marry, not him, but the terrible Hun.

> Je vous aime. Ce mot me coûte à prononcer;
> Mais puisqu'il vous plaît tant, je veux bien m'y forcer.

Permettez toutefois que je vous die encore
Que, si votre Attila de ce grand choix m'honore,
Je recevrai sa main d'un oeil aussi content
Que si je me donnais ce que mon coeur prétend:
Non que de son amour je ne prenne un tel gage
Pour le dernier supplice et le dernier outrage,
Et que le dur effort d'un si cruel moment
Ne redouble ma haine et mon ressentiment;
Mais enfin mon devoir veut une déférence
Où même il ne soupçonne aucune répugnance.
Je l'épouserai donc, et réserve pour moi
La gloire de répondre à ce que je me doi.
J'ai ma part, comme une autre, à la haine publique
Et le hais d'autant plus, que son ambition
A voulu s'asservir toute ma nation.

Mon amour, et ma haine, et la cause commune
Criront à la vengeance, en voudront trois pour une;
Et comme j'aurai lors sa vie entre mes mains
Il a lieu de me craindre autant que je vous plains,
Assez d'autres tyrans ont péri par leurs femmes;
Cette gloire aisément touche les grandes âmes,
Et de ce même coup qui brisera mes fers,
Il est beau que ma main venge tout l'univers.
Voilà quelle je suis, voilà ce que je pense,
Voilà ce que l'amour prépare à qui l'offense.
Vous, faites-moi justice; et songez mieux, seigneur,
S'il faut me dire encor que je manque de coeur.

The passage is typical; it is the poet, not at his rare best, but as he is to be found on every page. Nowhere does a line ever give the reader a moment's doubt as to the meaning. When he opens his Corneille, he need make no effort; the poet has done that for him.

When "all was without form and void, God said, Let there be light: and there was light." So Corneille saw his charge as a tragic poet. Over the formless void of dimly struggling, dumbly suffering mankind the artist throws light, and the chaos of reality gives way to the clarity of ordered thought.

Therefore to find Corneille one must leave the common meeting ground of the tragedians of other countries, where the Greeks are and Shakespeare, Goethe too, and Schiller perhaps, and a modern or so. There is a park marked "For Frenchmen Only," and here French tragedy abides. Into that place of beautiful order where elegance and the sublime of admiration dwell companionably together, there is no admission for pity or terror or wonder. The most intellectual nation in the world intellectualized tragedy, and in the process mystery was eliminated; the insoluble question tragedy elsewhere has always posed was dismissed as affording no ground for rational treatment. There was dropped out that which all men have experienced, but which no man understands.

GOETHE AND FAUST

Goethe's claims to greatness are many, but to the world at large he is a dramatist. His popular fame rests on *Faust*. It is a baffling play; it perplexes and disturbs.

There are two parts to the play. Once the first part was overshadowed by the second, which was studied as a deep philosophy expressed through enigmatic symbolism. Today it is read—at least outside of Germany—for its nature poetry, about the most beautiful there is, and the ironic, delightful figure of Mephistopheles. The symbolic philosophy has withdrawn to the background. The problem of *Faust* now is not what this or that symbol stands for, it is Faust himself.

The story of the play is familiar. Even the reader who comes to it for the first time knows the outline. Gretchen yields to Faust. He kills her mother unintentionally, her brother in self-defense, and leaves her and the city to save his life. She kills their child, is imprisoned and executed. The night before her execution Mephistopheles is forced by Faust to bring him to her in her prison cell. There he tells her that he has come to take her away with him. She says:

How is it that you do not shrink from me?
I have killed my mother and drowned my child.

He tells her, "Let the past be past or it will kill me." She
answers:

No, you must live—live on.
And I will tell you how the graves must lie.
The best place for my mother.
And next to her my brother.
With me apart, but not too far away.
The little one at my right breast.
And no one else will lie there near me.

He urges her again to come with him, but again she draws
back. In despair Faust cries that he will carry her away by
force. She says:

Not that. Not violence.
Once I gave all to my dear love.

He tells her they must hasten. The day breaks. She answers:

Day. Yes it is day. My last.
It should have been my wedding day—
We shall see each other once again
Where the crowd gathers silently
And I am seized and bound
For the red block—the block to which they lead me.
The steel quivers above me—
Then silence—silence like the grave.

At this moment Mephistopheles enters. Gretchen cries
out that she will not go with him. Mephistopheles sternly

bids Faust to come or he is lost. He disappears and astonishedly Faust follows him. He leaves Gretchen. Her voice is heard calling him twice by name. It dies away. The curtain falls. The first part of *Faust* is ended.

The naive reader opens the second part with throbbing expectation. What happened? Gretchen died, of course; the story is clear. But did Faust actually leave her to die alone? Or did he try to the very end to save her and fail? In either case his anguish must have reached to the very height of tragic pain. How will Goethe's immense power of poetry put that into words? Surely there will be some transcendent expression of the mystery of suffering as in *Lear* or in Greek tragedy.

As the first page is turned, a feeling of complete bewilderment comes. From a prison cell the reader is confronted with a hillside in the hush of dawn, where Faust lies asleep. Above him hover lovely spirits bidding him awake to the glory of the sunrise and the rapture of the new day. Beauty beckons to him from shadowy ravines and radiant heights. Glory and rapture take full possession of him.

A paradise above, beneath, lies round me.

Only a page back Gretchen's piteous figure was there, speaking words of almost unbearable pathos. Now she is gone as if she never had been. Her love, her misery, her death on the red block have vanished from her creator's mind. His hero is full of glowing zest for life and yet more life. It is as if after Desdemona's death the curtain rose on Othello eagerly bound for fresh journeys.

The second part of *Faust* is almost as long as *Paradise Lost*. On the last page "a penitent once called Gretchen" is with the angelic host who are escorting Faust to heaven. It is her only appearance.

What is the explanation of this strange refusal on the part of one of the world's greatest writers to complete what he began with such power of truth and beauty? No character in literature surpasses Gretchen in point of pathos. But Goethe turned away from her so decisively that he did not allow one thought of her ever again to enter Faust's mind. Apparently it never occurred to him that Faust might thereby forfeit the reader's sympathy. The play says beyond the possibility of doubt that Goethe thought leaving Gretchen to die and forgetting her was entirely comprehensible.

But for a very great poet to think thus is not comprehensible. No other great poet ever did. If the records of Goethe's life were as meager as those of Shakespeare's, the puzzle would remain forever unsolved. But we know much about Goethe, and to read his life is to understand Faust.

"Il ne faut pas toucher aux idoles. La dorure en reste aux mains." Goethe is the outstanding example of the truth of Flaubert's words. He has been so much handled, a great deal of the gilding has come off. Partly it is that he was a German, the greatest German of them all. The whole weight of German scholarship was laid upon him.

Even in his lifetime he suffered. Eagerly listening, conscientiously painstaking men accompanied him on his walks or his drives or his tea parties to catch with rapt attention each remark that fell from his lips, and to write it down, no matter how cheerfully inept, every night in the privacy of their chambers with reverent accuracy. And all they wrote down has been studied and annotated and studied again until the text looks insignificant beside the commentary.

His very love letters, when this formidable thoroughness is applied to them, turn into impressive documents where the expressions of endearment seem as unsuitable as if one found them in a dictionary.

"I must bid my beloved good night by a returning postillion, which she will receive as a good morning. We arrived in rain."

NOTE: This time he was going with Knebel and Fritz to Ilmenau, but not, as he had once planned, by way of Jena. They left by the road which was commonly used by those departing from Weimar.

"Think of me, dearest. The evening was lost for us."

NOTE: This could hardly be the evening lost because of Seckendorf's departure—who, however, did go away the next morning. Knebel, too, left Weimar on the 16th. He met Seckendorf in Jena, who was traveling to Bayreuth.

"Farewell, dearest. Accompany me with your thoughts. How delightful it was to me yesterday to see your face again. Keep me in remembrance, beloved. The weather promises well."

NOTE: Where Goethe was going on this occasion cannot be discovered. There are no indications of a visit to Jena. It is true that Scholl places this letter in 1784, not 1785, but there, too, at this date, May 11th, there is no suggestion to be found of any journey. I have therefore left it where Mscr. places it.

It is hard on Goethe. But he drew it down upon himself. He never would play the role of idol, and he did not care in the very least about gilding. If he could have foreseen the present appearance of his love letters, he would not have felt a moment's concern.

He enjoyed talking, and it did not diminish—or enhance —his enjoyment to have a dull man follow him about and record every word in his immense notebook. He would often laugh at Eckermann, yet without a thought of guarding himself against that solemn tenacity. No reader of Boswell but wonders at Dr. Johnson's powers of living up to expectation without ever relaxing. We shall never know how much we owe the biographer not only for recording the great man, but for bringing him about. Certainly Dr. Johnson would not have uttered all those admirable sayings— or refrained from uttering what would not be admirable— without his omnipresent worshipper.

Not so Goethe. He would talk exactly as he pleased without the slightest considerations for posterity; write his letters just as he happened to feel at the moment; jot down perfectly uninspired items in his notebook, unaware, to be sure, of the microscopic eyes which were to scan them hereafter. Nevertheless, if he had been ever so aware, the result would have been the same. He would unquestionably have been amused; he would not have been one iota more discreet. What he knew about life and nature and mankind he did care to hand on in an imperishable and unassailable form, but what sort of figure he would cut to future generations was never in his mind at all.

He was quite willing to discuss his love affairs, and his biographers have fallen upon them with enthusiasm. He had a large number; more than a dozen are on record, very full record, what with all that Goethe said about them and all his friends added and all the scholars after them discovered. But in spite of reams written on the subject, not one of them adds anything to our understanding of Goethe except the fact that he always ran away as soon as the possibility of being responsible for the beloved creature loomed darkly ahead of him. Except once, in the case of his very strange marriage, he was always terrorized and took himself off as fast as he could. The affair with Frau von Stein lasted, indeed, ten years; but then Frau von Stein was married and a member of the court circle at Weimar. There was never any question of her divorcing her husband and marrying Goethe. In point of fact, it was an ideal situation for him: he could love as much as he pleased without seeing any threat to his freedom. And in the end he ran away from her too. He was being bored. Not as bad as being married, but suggestive enough of that state to be alarming.

This flight motif is developed nowhere better than in the affair with Frederike Brion. When Goethe visited her, he found himself in surroundings that seemed to him, he writes, just like those in *The Vicar of Wakefield:* her family showed him the same unsuspicious kindliness; he was treated like a son by the simple, unworldly parson and his wife; he stayed with them for weeks at a time. He writes at length about them in his autobiography, where, however, the wary reader is always on his guard. It was written when he was an old man, and once discussing it with Eckermann he told him, "Everything described really took place, but nothing precisely as it is described." According to his story there, he instantly fell in love with Frederike, one of the daughters. "I was happy beyond all bounds at her side," he says. "We lived only for each other." Then later, in words that have an ominous sound, "It was thought that perfect confidence could be placed in my rectitude. We were left unobserved." The final parting, inevitable since Goethe was Goethe, comes as suddenly and unexpectedly to the reader as it did to the poor Frederike. One brief paragraph in the autobiography disposes of it.

My passionate connection with Frederike began to trouble me. I went to see her less frequently. She knew how to bring her situation before me with cheerfulness, and I called her merits to mind with fervour and with passion. At such moments I could blind myself to the future, but finally all became too confused as is always the case when one is to free oneself from a place. I could not fail to see her once more. Those were painful days, the memory of which has not remained with me. When I reached her my hand from my horse, tears were in her eyes, and I felt very uneasy.

Frederike had many successors. Goethe was only twenty-two when he left her, and for the rest of his life, some sixty years, he continued to be in love. "It is a very pleasant feeling," he writes, "when a new passion begins to stir before the old has disappeared."

It is true that he finally married, but a woman who had been his mistress for eighteen years. Their seventeen-year-old son was one of the witnesses of the marriage. It is hardly to be doubted that he took this dreaded step because she saved his life during the French invasion of Jena. When in other years she had wept because of slights offered her as his mistress, he would sit by, he wrote, silent and ashamed; but his shame never drove him to do anything more about it than write a poem on the pathos of her situation. His gratitude, however, did. The wedding took place a few days after she had disposed of the French troopers who were threatening him. Goethe was grateful, but hardly resigned. "Marriage," he said, "which must be preserved in the interest of social order, is essentially abnormal."

His wife happened to be a good-humored, compliant woman who made him comfortable and had enough good sense not to be disagreeable when he would go away to live by himself sometimes for months at a time, or when she would hear of an affair with this or that woman. Before he married her he had been faithful to her so far as we know, and it seems we know everything. Immediately after, he was unfaithful. If he could not have his freedom in one way, he would have it in another. The marriage lasted up to her death, eight years later. Within a month or so after that he was making love to a pretty child of nineteen, a daughter of one of his friends.

As an old man, looking back over his life, he said that there was only one woman he had ever really loved—not as one would expect, his first love, the sweet, cheerful Frederike, or his longest love, Frau von Stein of the eighteen hundred love letters, but Lili Schönemann, who was the only woman he ever engaged himself to marry. He was then about twenty-five, and she was a pretty, popular girl, moving in a circle rather superior to that of Goethe's family. But her people as well as his own and all their friends gave them their blessing; Lili was ready; there was no obstacle except the ardent lover himself. Goethe suddenly went off to Weimar and never came back. A short time before, he had written a friend about his exalted joy at Lili's side, "the most solemnly sweet situation of all my life. Through glowing tears of love the world and all about me appears full of soul." In Weimar a few months later he had a letter: "I read in a sort of stupor, Lili is married. Then I turned around and went to sleep. How I blessed Fate's dealings." He had already been for some time at Frau von Stein's feet. This, on Goethe's own authority, was the great passion of his life.

The truth is, of course, that he never really loved any woman. He felt a tolerant affection born of long habit for the woman he finally made his wife who never interfered with him, and he had a good many attacks of passion which could be accurately reckoned if it were not for some women in Italy whose identity as well as whose number has so far eluded the scholars. But as far as the Italian women themselves are concerned, they are all unimportant to the student of Goethe. They did nothing to him. He would have been exactly the same if he had never known any of them.

Once only, when he was around thirty, he met one who was really a noteworthy personage. She was the Marchesa Branconi, a great lady, as famous for her intelligence as for her beauty. "What would not that woman make of a man," he said. But the very force of the attraction she had for him made him draw back. "She would drag my soul out of my body," he wrote. Goethe's soul was not for anyone.

His relations with his family fit perfectly into the picture. One's family has a way of becoming one's responsibility, and this Goethe would not have, any more than in the case of the women he fell in love with. Frankfurt, where his parents lived, was no great distance from Weimar even in those days of coaches and post-horses, but he let years pass without going to see them, and he would never let them come to see him. There was no break ever, no quarrel. That was not Goethe's way. He writes of them invariably with complete good-will, even affection. "From my little mother (came) my happy disposition and love of story telling. . . . I had in her an incomparable companion." A pleasant picture, but when he went to Frankfurt in 1792, he had not seen her for thirteen years, in the course of which his father had died. She was left quite alone, and wanted to move to Weimar. Goethe would not hear of it. He even refused a kindly offer from the Dowager Duchess of Weimar to invite her for a visit. Once he offered to receive her, not long before her death, when the French were threatening to invade Frankfurt, but by that time she would not come.

It was the same with his only sister—he had no brothers. He writes of her, too, with marked affection. "We shared and endured all things hand in hand. . . . Whenever I was ill, she devoted all her time to caring for me." But when she fell ill and lay dying, he did not go to her.

His letter to his mother at the time suggests that he perceived a need to excuse himself. It was a stupid excuse, and Goethe was not given to stupidity. Nevertheless, it is true that every egotist, no matter how greatly endowed, can on occasion be stupid in a way impossible to completely commonplace people whose center of interest admits others besides themselves. The blind spot of egotism obscured Goethe's vision when he, all that was now left to his sorrowing mother, wrote her that by now he had grown to feel just as Christ felt when his mother and brethren wished to see him, and he turned to his disciples and said, "Behold my mother and my brethren."

Friends, of course, fared no better. One of his oldest and dearest, whose house was in the same street as his, sent him a message when he was dying to beg him to come and bid him good-bye; but all he got in answer was a little note.

No one who has read as far as this in the story of his life feels any surprise that he let his mother die alone. It is clear that one thing he would not put up with was any attendance upon a sickbed or deathbed, no matter who lay on it. There should be nothing astonishing either in the fact that when she died, he had not seen her for more than eleven years. People who loved him always ended by being an intolerable trial to him. And yet no mother ever demanded less.

Some years before she died, Frau von Stein's little son, a boy of twelve, came to her for a visit and made great friends with her. From that time on, she wrote touching letters to the boy in which she showed her love and longing for her own son. "Since you are constantly with my son," one begins, "how would it be if you were to keep a little diary and send it to me? It need not be much—only something like this. 'Yesterday Goethe was at the play; in the evening he was invited out.' So I could live, as it were, among you." And again: "The diary is just what I wanted. It has brought me great joy. Now the separation from my son will be easier for me because I shall see through your writing all that is done in Weimar as if I were there."

But to Goethe she never showed what she was feeling, not once in all the letters she wrote him. She never so much as asked him to come and see her. She kept assuring him that she was happy. Her last letter, written shortly before she died, is full of the sweetest gaiety as well as of tender affection. It is a delightful letter. She describes how much pleasure she still gets from her inveterate habit of telling stories and how people enjoy them just as much as ever they did. She is very proud, too, of her wonderful son, but not conceited enough to think that she had anything to do with making him great. There is not a hint of the eleven years

since she last saw him, not a suggestion of any hurt feeling.
One reads the letter incredulously, and yet it is precisely the
sort of thing Goethe would have written her if their situa-
tions had been reversed. Here at any rate they saw life in the
same way. "Let us have nothing unpleasant." That was
fundamental to both of them. We are told of her that
whenever she engaged a servant, she would say, "You are
not to tell me of anything distressing or disturbing, whether
it happens in my own house or in the town. If it concerns
me, I shall know it soon enough." No one would have had
to explain that attitude to Goethe.

Her technique was his own. He used it throughout his
life, with friends and enemies alike. It enabled him to live
pleasantly and peacefully with his mistress during the eighteen years before he married her. She was, to be sure, a
humble and undemanding creature as well as cheerful and
sweet-tempered, but she was without training or education,
a factory worker when he first met her, and her ways and his
were far apart. He did not try to impose his upon her. He
left her free to do as she pleased: to dance all night when she
wished, to go to the theatre with a train of noisy young men,
to drink too much in public places. He never remonstrated,
he was never out of humor with her. He let her fill the house,
too, with her extremely undesirable relatives, so full sometimes that there was no peace or privacy for him. Of course
he could always go away. He kept quarters in Jena and
sometimes stayed there for months. He would have liberty
for himself, but he gave it to her no less. By some strange
twisted reasoning he held that each of them was free of the
other because they were not married. He held to that idea
through eighteen years of living together.

The most remarkable instance of his power to live with

people on his own terms is the way he dealt with his son, the only child of his who lived to grow up. He was illegitimate, of course, and cut off from a boy's ordinary life. It is on record that other children taunted him with his birth. He was a difficult lad, too, and his mother was quite incapable of training him. What might not his father be obliged to do for him? Goethe seemed at last terrifyingly faced with having to take responsibility for someone he could not run away from, and someone who bade fair to be exceedingly troublesome. It was a situation full of danger for his tranquility. Perhaps it went even deeper than that. He had been very fond of the boy when he was a little child, and perhaps that cool, powerful mind saw that there were potentialities of pain for him there, even great pain, if he continued to care for him. At all events, Goethe's biographers agree that he drew back decisively. He succeeded in becoming indifferent. The lad was left entirely to his mother, and he and his father lived together as strangers.

He came to a bad end while he was still young, a drunkard's death, a relief by that time to everyone connected with him. His mother had died years before, and his wife lived on with Goethe and kept his house. She was a trivial and trying person, and her two boys were troublesome, undisciplined children; but Goethe got on perfectly with them all, in his own way. If the lads' tutor came to report some misdeed, their grandfather would stroke his chin and say reflectively, "Ah." Further than that he would not go and one concludes that the misdeeds did not long continue to be reported. He dealt with his daughter-in-law in much the same fashion. Once when she fell from her horse and cut her face badly, he refused to go near her until the wound was healed. On the other hand, whenever she was more than usually incompetent, he would quietly fill up her deficiencies. Everything came easily to him, even house-keeping. He liked to make both ends meet. Always he was gentle and sweet-tempered to mother and children, imperturbably pleasant.

He was able to live contentedly with them for years. Such as they were they could not touch him personally. They would never make him care for them and suffer through them. He did not have to protect himself from them or ever run away.

In his autobiography he speaks of "my infinite good-will, my universal benevolence which prompted me to lend my active aid to all." This is not a piece of conceit. Goethe had far less than his share of that quality. The statement must be qualified, but there is much truth in it. He did have infinite good-will when no danger threatened his peace of mind.

He closed his heart to his son, but he took endless pains to turn the wayward boy who was absolute master of Weimar into a wise and good ruler. He would not lift a finger for his parents, but from the time he was twenty-six until he was thirty-six he gave up his own work and put all his powers at the disposal of the little Weimar state. During those ten years his activity was purely beneficent. He reformed the finances, made over the roads, devised fire protection for isolated villages, inspection for factories, and so on. He devoted himself tirelessly to tedious and perplexing and forever pressing business details. He wrote: "I have to screw myself up afresh every day; a thousand big things and little things to be put through. I keep imagination out of the business—only want to know what there is to know and get things done."

He would take any amount of trouble for his friends, too —except when they lay ill or dying. He welcomed Schiller to Weimar and produced his plays eagerly—he had taken on the direction of the theatre by then. The fact that they were applauded, as his own never were, made no difference. He felt only delight in their great success; he brought them out again and again. No friend ever came to him in need of encouragement or money and went away disappointed, but no friend was ever allowed to come near enough to make his troubles Goethe's own.

His letters to his mother were few and cold, but he wrote often and with tender compassion to an anonymous protégé, a morbid, difficult person whom he secretly supported up to his death—and Goethe's means were never large. What he gave away was at the cost of his own comfort and ease. "Believe me," one letter begins, "you are not a burden to me; on the contrary, you teach me economy. And do you think your thanks are nothing? He who has can give, he cannot thank." All the letters to this man are written with the same delicacy of feeling. He never spoke to anyone of his charities. "Men suffer," he wrote Frau von Stein, "and one is ashamed to feel oneself favored above so many. God grant me to be more economical that I may do more for others." Once when he was trying to finish *Iphigenia*, he could not go on writing "because of the misery of the stocking-weavers at Apolda."

He was right in claiming general benevolence for himself. He could be moved to compassion and to self-denial for the unfortunate. But when another's pain threatened pain to him, he could harden his heart against any touch of compassion.

This strange shift from great kindness to great unkindness

has engaged the attention of his critics and his adorers, but the truth is that the contradiction is apparent only, not real. Goethe was a singularly consistent character. He knew what he wanted from life and he allowed nothing to interfere with his securing it. His *summum bonum* was serenity of spirit and he achieved it in an extraordinary measure.

His famous doctrine of renunciation is nothing more than a logical and very practical means to avoid disturbing the inner calm. "Renounce," he writes. "You must renounce." This is not renunciation in the great sense. Stevenson's, "To renounce without bitterness," which, he tells us, "is a task to engage all a man's strength." That kind of renunciation is positive, it must be fought for; it is the result of self-conquest. Goethe's, on the contrary, was negative; it was won by yielding; as he shows over and over again in his life and in his writings, its motive was self-protection. "It is better," he says, "to relinquish once for all than to be forever in a rage about yesterday, today, tomorrow."

As far as a human being can, he put suffering away from him. He opened his heart to compassion for others, but he refused to suffer for others, and, as he perceived unerringly, he had therefore to keep everyone at a distance—family, friends, lovers. He had meditated much on Spinoza. As far as he could follow anyone he was a follower of his. "Except," writes Spinoza, "on account of that which is the object of love no contentions can arise; there can be no sorrow, no fear; in short, no disturbance of mind."

One sees Goethe reading the words with a flash of illumination. The truth pierced the very heart of life's engima. The love of individual human beings, life's best gift, and suffering, life's hardest gift, went hand in hand. One could not accept the one without taking upon oneself the other also. The only way to love without danger, Spinoza declared, to love with never a pang of pain to trouble the spirit, was "to give love to that which is eternal and infinite, to that which alone causes joy untainted by any sorrow." That was the way Goethe could love, secure in the infinite and eternal against the anguish which is the lot of those who love through sickness and through sin, through danger and through death, individual people in this finite and temporal world.

Schiller, who alone of the men Goethe knew was fitted by his own genius to understand him, wrote, "He binds men to him by small as well as by great attentions, but he always knows how to hold himself free—like a god, without giving himself."

He never gave himself. He never really suffered. He lived serenely aloof like Spinoza's God, whom men must love, but not expect to love them.

There will always be men to commend this remarkable achievement, hardly to be paralleled in human annals, the result of an unwavering resolution to avoid pain and complete clarity of mind to perceive the one sure way. The extent of Goethe's work may well have thus been made possible, his long life with unimpaired powers to the very end. But there will always be others to maintain that this surpassing genius, power of intellect and power of poetry combined as in hardly another, refused "the great initiation." That refusal made *Faust* what it is. Goethe turned away from the tragic heights Faust might have trod, and he never saw to what low levels he made him sink.

SELECTED
BOOK REVIEWS

The World of Plato

This is the most illuminating book I have ever read on Greece.* I found myself wishing as I laid down the second volume of Gilbert Highet's translation—the third and last is not yet translated—that it could be required reading for all the multitudes today who are drawing up schemes for a new world. This is not only because I am a lover of the Greeks and have had the keenest pleasure in Professor Jaeger's at once profound and lucid exposition of the depths and heights they reached. Professor Jaeger is more than a scholar in the high sense of the word, a disinterested seeker of the truth endowed with mental equipment adequate for the search: he is a man of great wisdom. Wisdom is not the same as knowledge and it is different from learning: its concern is always men. And Professor Jaeger's primary interest is human beings; he has a deep understanding of their ways.

In consequence, he has written a new kind of book. It

* Werner Jaeger, *Paideia, The Ideals of Greek Culture*, Vols. I and II, translated by Gilbert Highet. New York: Oxford University Press, 1944.

might seem natural that only one who knew and cared for human nature would write about Greek or any other culture, since culture is a purely human product, but the reverse is so often true that this book is a startling novelty. Like many historians, whose subject is the actions of men, but who know little and care less what men really are, so writers on art and theology and politics and economics tend to drop from their consideration the puzzling creatures who are responsible for producing them. They like to discuss each as a thing in itself, a proper subject for discussion in proportion as it is separated from its origin.

Professor Jaeger's method is the exact opposite. His study of Greek literature is a human document. *Paideia*, the title he gives it, is a Greek word hard to translate. Culture, the common translation, is a word so misused by now that we instinctively avoid it. To the Greek, *paideia* stood for education and training, together with the result of them—"the shaping of the Greek character," Professor Jaeger calls it.

The first volume traces the course of this shaping process from Homer to the end of the fifth century, and—since for human nature that which hath been is that which shall be —we find our modern selves in its pages. Not that Professor Jaeger ever compares past and present. He never says a word about today, but, nevertheless, he writes for today. As when he tells of the Greek theatre, how the early plays had been valued as great expressions of great truths, but "now they are prized only as mediums for the actor; acting had come to dominate the stage; it had conquered poetry. Not form and content, but histronic effect was supreme."

In the second volume, devoted to Socrates and Plato, the implicit comparison is more forceful. Professor Jaeger shows the changelessness of truth, the eternal verity of what Socrates, the master, exemplified in his life, and Plato, his pupil, put into words.

The two, among the greatest minds and spirits that have ever lived, were faced by imminent fundamental changes in the life of their times, and they set themselves to think out how it could be rescued from the materialism that had infected it and be enabled to run its course in freedom and happiness.

Socrates' search for the truth was based solidly upon the facts of human life, since human nature is the part of the world best known to us and so the surest clue to understanding it. His teaching never became a system of abstract thought which could be considered apart from his own self. In its briefest form it is: "What shall it profit a man if he gain the whole world and lose his soul?" Like one who lived four hundred years later, he never wrote anything down, not a single word. He only talked, with an intense interest in each man he met, to arouse him to seek the good. He was himself the embodiment of what he taught. A hero of the moral life, he died for the truth.

Plato put into words what Socrates lived. He thought it through, and to this day, Professor Jaeger says, the character of any philosophy is determined by its relation to Plato. Do not fear in this book any long bewildering discussions of the Platonic Ideas. Professor Jaeger sees Plato's thought as the framework of his faith; his problem the same as Socrates', how men are to become better; his contribution, the reasoned statement of the new standard of values Socrates had exemplified in his life and death.

The shaken world Plato lived in could not, he declared, be re-established by any outside authority; it must begin in each citizen's soul. Each man must master himself, the only part of the world peculiarly his own. For this he must be trained by teachers who knew that the work of educating was the service of God and the power to know the good the profoundest force in mankind. All so educated would be friends, and friendship is the only form of productive connection between men. Their leader would be the true statesman, never yielding to the mob to please and flatter, but devoted to the single aim of making his fellow-citizens better. He could do so because the foundation of the true statesman's power is the power of the truth to convince. The state's chief function was through the statesman to train the individual and so set him free, since freedom is inner discipline. The absence of discipline is the shortest way to the loss of liberty. The logical end of democracy, which contains the maximum of liberty, is tyranny. A contest inevitably arises between the rich and the workers. The result is a tyrant, the champion of the one or the other, usually the latter as they are most numerous. In either case the end is despair. The people realize finally they are the slaves of a monster, for that is what a tyrant always becomes. Absolute power corrupts absolutely. The tyrant, too, is a slave, enslaved by fear, by his mistrust of everyone. As Aeschylus said:

> There is a sickness that infects all tyrants,
> They cannot trust their friends.

So he ends the most miserable and the loneliest of all men on earth. Over against him is the true citizen whose Republic does not yet exist anywhere except in the souls of men. But he who realizes that divine order in himself makes the great contribution toward bringing it into actual existence.

Human truths once seen and expressed never die; they are always valid. We take that for granted in reading the Bible, but toward other ancient books we are apt to be condescending. But no one who reads Professor Jaeger's book will ever again be condescending to the truths that began to live in Greece three thousand years ago.

Born Under a Rhyming Planet

The question to be answered before a translation can be appraised is, what ought a translation to be? The answer is not easy.

I have read with great pleasure Professor Murray's translation of *The Seven Against Thebes*.* It is not only written with the exquisite taste and the sensitive feeling that mark all his work, it is also astonishingly spirited. The description of the Seven and the champions Thebes opposed to them is a stirring piece of writing, a very paean of war. I am lost in surprise as well as admiration. Never would I have thought that Professor Murray could turn himself into a bard of such a martial lay. Indeed of all Greek tragedies I would have supposed this embattled drama the one least suited to his gifts. But now that I have read what he has done with it, I like it better than any other of his translations, even than his *Trojan Women*, which has hitherto seemed to me his best. It is greatly superior to his *Agamemnon*. The language is simpler and more direct; it is

* Aeschylus, *The Seven Against Thebes*, translated by Gilbert Murray. New York: Oxford University Press, 1935.

not so besprinkled with "yea" and "lo" and "mayhap" and the like, nor with the old *th* ending which appears continually in the *Agamemnon*, not always with the happiest result:

> There abideth in wrath reawoken—
> It plotteth, it haunteth the house, yea, it never forgetteth.

There is nothing like that in this version of the "Seven." It has vigor; it is often lively and sometimes warm and glowing. It is interesting from first to last. Of what other translation from the Greek can that be said?

And yet here the critic pauses. If this were Professor Murray's own work—but it is not. How is it to be judged as a translation? What ought a translation to be?

Few will say that it should be completely literal. Du Maurier showed once and for all the perils which attend that ideal:

> *Cassez-vous, cassez-vous, cassez-vous,*
> *sur vos froids gris cailloux, O mer.*

"As faithful as it can, as free as it must," is a German critic's answer, but he leaves us to define for ourselves what is faithfulness, precisely the point the whole matter turns upon. Professor Murray would define it, I think, as first of all the quality by virtue of which a translation gets over the footlights. He would say that there could be no greater infidelity to Aeschylus than to turn his play into something dull and dead. To make the reader bored by Greek tragedy would be to betray the cause he has so signally championed of saving Greek literature for an age that does not read Greek. Therefore, whenever the original seems to him calculated to put the reader off, he stops translating to rewrite. He anglicizes an idea as well as a phrase:

> God's anger passeth by the poor;
> Only the princes of the world
> Uprooted to the void are cast.

That familiar contrast between the righteous poor and the wicked rich does not come to us from the Greek, but from the English Bible. The Greeks never saw it that way. In the passage quoted, the first line is not in the original. Aeschylus does not speak of the poor. Professor Murray adds the words to make the reader feel comfortably at home.

It is Aeschylus' way only to suggest the emotional appeal in a situation. So when he writes of girls captured at the sack of a town, his words are sober and unemphatic: "Piteous for those of tender age plucked unripe, before the customary rite, to tread the hateful road away from home." But Professor Murray feels that he must make sure that the reader appreciates all the pathos:

> Weep, weep for the torn flower,
> The flower of maidenhood, the trodden grass
> Ravished before its hour.
> Away to a strange dwelling place they pass
> Hating each step.

As this passage shows, the translation is rhymed throughout. Professor Murray was born under a rhyming planet. Tennyson and Swinburne were the masters of his youth. Small wonder that he learned to love rhyme. But odd things do happen to the rhyming translator. Professor Murray makes Eteocles say, "An ever-sleepless pilot, hand on oar," the reason for this unnautical statement being that "oar" is to rhyme with "therefor." Aeschylus never turned his pilot into an oarsman. He wrote "rudder." Such carping criticism apart, one cannot escape the fact that if one must rhyme as well as translate, some attention must be diverted from the translation. But Professor Murray is thinking only of commending Aeschylus to the reader by what he elsewhere calls the rhyme's ringing quality.

The rich rhyming speech of the great Victorian poets is always in his ears. It makes him fear that Antigone will sound bald and unbeautiful to English readers when Aeschylus makes her say:

> No one shall ever thus decree for me.
> I am a woman and yet will I make
> A grave, a burying, for him—
> Carry the earth in my cloak's linen fold
> With my own hands to cover him.

The swift words are turned into smooth-flowing rhyming couplets:

> Let none believe it! I myself will lay
> His limbs in earth, and, woman though I be
> Heap o'er him the grave's covering canopy.
> Aye, though I find but what these hands can hold
> Of earth within my mantle's linen fold.

Few translations are long-lived. It has been truly said that the translations of former generations are from a dead language into a dead language. We need someone to do for us today what Professor Murray once did with such notable success. He made Greek live for his contemporaries. But another idiom is needed now for that miracle. Only let the

new translator take to heart the words of another true
Grecian, Gildersleeve, that a translation can be only an
etching of a great painting, "and, in the Muses' name, do
not color an etching."

A Tottering World

The Age of Constantine is one of the best known works
of the distinguished Swiss historian, Jakob Burckhardt.*
Written in the nineteenth century, it is now offered in
English for the first time in an admirable translation by
Moses Hadas.

The subject of the book, which is that of some of the
most famous chapters in Gibbon, makes a comparison inevitable, but Burckhardt's spirit has nothing in common
with that of the most ironical of historians. For example, he
says that Juvenal's scoffing at the animal worship in Egypt
"might be read with pleasure if the shadowy outline of
the oldest civilization on earth did not possess something
venerable which we do not willingly see trodden in the
dust."

This is the spirit in which Burckhardt surveys the spectacle of a supremely great civilization dying of old age. He
assembles compassionately the signs of senility and holds
up a mirror for future ages.

In this picture of a tottering world the political situation
has an appearance of well-being. It had clarified in the
hands of two strong men, Diocletian and Constantine.

* Jakob Burckhardt, *The Age of Constantine the Great*, translated by
Moses Hadas. New York: Pantheon Books, 1949.

Republican forms, long obsolete, were finally cast aside. No consul ruled the state, but the Lord Emperor. The Senate still deliberated in weighty, dignified debates, but its sole charge was to ratify the laws the Emperor proposed.

Economic troubles were multiplying. The bureaucracy had increased enormously, the expenses likewise, and of course the taxes. Burckhardt says a writer of the period remarked that when the proportion of those who receive money exceeds the proportion of those who contribute, taxation became intolerable.

Diocletian, Constantine's forerunner in empire-building, established ceiling prices in an effort to lighten the burden, but the result was that goods were hidden, even destroyed, and higher prices demanded and accepted. It was reported that a certain official had said he would use wine to slake lime rather than reduce the price. The populace set his house on fire. Finally the law was rescinded.

Its passage was an indication of the Government's paternal solicitude, undreamed of in Rome of the Republic. Poor families could get a grant from the state; far-flung irrigation works were undertaken; agriculture was protected: even private morals were a public concern. Signs of old age? Burckhardt thinks it quite possible.

Freedom was lost irretrievably. Beauty was following suit. Architecture's aim was toward the big, the bigger and the biggest. The painters turned to the symbolic: they strove to express general ideas, abstractions. Art was becoming more and more the handmaid of state propaganda.

Literature was chiefly collections and critical estimates. With the poets words were often regarded as an end in themselves and amazing elaborations resulted. Governmental literature was a law unto itself. Big-sounding words and circumlocutions were its specialty.

In religion as nowhere else appeared "the new needs of the old world." Burckhardt points out that inevitably as the individual's natural energy to overcome obstacles disappeared along with his independence, he cried out for a support. A wave of credulity swept over the land. Magic ruled, its reign not disputed even by the Christians or the Jews.

Constantine, claimed by many churchly historians as a sincere convert to Christianity, has another aspect to the Swiss historian. It is, of course, incontestable that at the great Council of Nicaea he took a decisive part in determining the exact constitution of the Trinity, but it is no less incontestable that within three years of championing what was to become the cornerstone of orthodoxy, he murdered his eldest son, drowned his wife in her bath, and had his eleven-year-old nephew put to death. An inadequate conversion, Burckhardt comments.

The book is timely. It is to be wished that it will be widely read. The Roman Empire merits a look from those who do not think human nature a constant. Burckhardt has the power to present specific facts so that a general truth emerges. In his hands the Age of Constantine becomes a picture of Empire, forever rising and falling through history.

Word From New Zion

Martin Buber's *Israel and the World* is a remarkable book.* Its subtitle is "Essays in a Time of Crisis," and it consists of articles and addresses on widely different subjects, all

* Martin Buber, *Israel and the World*. New York: Farrar, Straus & Young, 1948.

connected because their background is the new venture of
the Jews in Palestine.

It can fairly be divided into two parts. The first half is
an expression of what St. James calls "pure religion and
undefiled." There are very few books which belong to this
category. Devotional books, theological books, didactic religious books are without number, but pure religion has
had few expressions. And even where it is to be found one
must oftenest cull it out carefully from a host of matter
which has nothing to do with what is truly and purely religion. Almost all religious writers are so conditioned by
their creeds and their theologies that their books are largely
made up of emphatic, even passionate, statements of the
separation of the elect who accept the form or ritual or
dogma they advocate from the vast number of those who
do not.

But Professor Buber, although he writes as a Jew to Jews
from the Hebrew University of Palestine, is not concerned
with anything that goes on in synagogues or Jewish theological schools. He quotes what Moses said in Sinai to the
people who had listened to God: "Ye heard the voice of
words, but ye saw no form," and he comments, "It does
not matter what you call the voice. All that matters is that
you hear it."

He loves his own religion and he follows it with devo-
tion. It is God's way for him, but his book is no apologia
for it. He has reached a level, higher than Newman's,
where stand all those who see the light of God so clearly
that their eyes are blinded to the sharply drawn lines of
division, supremely important on the lower levels. "The
eternal truth," Professor Buber writes, "one of whose rays
has entered the teaching of Israel." That is a wonderful

declaration. In Palestine, where ardent Judaism is on the alert, combatting foes that would put it down, where two mighty forces—religion and nationalism—have united to put the foes down, in that atmosphere of passionate fervor a Jew says to his countrymen, "The eternal truth has myriads of rays. One of them has come to us."

An English writer in the early Middle Ages said, "God may well be loved. He cannot be thought." Over the centuries the modern Jew stretches out his hand to the medieval Christian. Professor Buber says, "God is found not by thought, but by love." Two rays of the eternal truth converge and double their brightness. There is an actuality, Professor Buber writes, which rises above the highest idea, and he quotes a great disciple of Kant, Hermann Cohen: "I can comprehend the ideal only by loving it." This is a declaration of the primacy of love in seeking the truth. The goal is not the knowledge of God, but the love of God. Love can give understanding beyond the understanding of the mind. St. John summed it up: "He that loveth not knoweth not God."

The philosophers' God is an idea, the Absolute, "a power," in Buber's words, "which cannot be identified with any attribute accessible to the human understanding." It is the loftiest image of all the images formed by the mind, but it is only an image, a human construction. "At the point, however, where the Absolute is loved," Buber says, "he is no longer the Absolute, but God."

What is the love of God? What does it mean to love God? Buber quotes an Athenian who said of the Jews, "They imitate God's mercy." The ways of God are "merciful, long-suffering, abundant in loving kindness and faithfulness." They are God's ways; they can be our ways. "Let the words of my mouth and the meditation of my heart be acceptable in Thy sight, O Lord."

The last half of the book is of less general interest. It discusses special problems for the people in Palestine, yet in a way that has nothing of narrow sectarianism. At the very end Buber says of the voice which speaks to Israel, the ray from the eternal truth which has come to them, that it is not the voice of a God whom the people created in their own image, but one who confronts them and makes a stern demand on them. He demands for the whole life of man, not for isolated spheres, truth and not lies, right and not wrong, so that the obligation to be truthful and to be just is for public as for private life, for the nation toward other nations as for the individual toward other individuals. Right is divided from wrong as unconditionally as when at the Creation God divided light from darkness.

Professor Buber's spirit is so elevated, his power to see the general in the particular is so great, that what he says to Jews in Asia any Christian can apply to Christianity in America.

This Will Never Do

To the Editor of the SATURDAY REVIEW

Sir: I have been so struck by the great significance of Mr. Rascoe's *Titans of Literature* * that although I cannot claim

* Burton Rascoe, *Titans of Literature*. New York: G. P. Putnam's Sons, 1932. Miss Hamilton's remarks were published as a Letter to the Editor.

to have more than an amateur's acquaintance with any
part of his vast subject except the chapters on Greek and
Latin, and must, therefore, confine myself to these alone,
nevertheless I am venturing to call your attention to the
real reason for the importance of his book, which so far
the critics seem not to have commented upon.

It is no less than a triumph of democracy so signal, it may
well prove to be the culmination of our ideal. For democracy, of course, rests upon the belief in the average man as
against the expert. This is the chief article in our creed.
Every trial by jury is an exemplification of our faith in
ordinary men. So, too, we choose our rulers: we, the untrained, choose the untrained to decide for us economic
questions which are to determine prosperity or misery for
us all. We have an instinctive distrust for the far-sought
conclusions of the expert, and an unshakable confidence in
the immediate good sense of men just like ourselves.

These are, of course, the mere commonplaces of democracy. It has remained for Mr. Rascoe to carry us a step
further, a step so great as to minimize all previous advances.
He has stormed the ancient, undemocratic, privileged cita-
del of the scholar and the critic and has handed it over to
democracy triumphant. The common-sense conclusions of
the men who wield the power in jury box and voting booth
are now the court of appeal before which scholar and critic
stand discredited.

A poor, shabby lot they are as Mr. Rascoe shows them
up, "humbugs," by and large, and "pettifogging obscurant-
ists," all in a conspiracy to trick the world into believing
that they have in their learning a unique possession which
the rest of us cannot share—a completely undemocratic
pretension, amounting indeed to no less than a claim to

special privileges.

But Mr. Rascoe in a few pages completely demolishes it. To begin with, so he assures us, the scholars really are not learned, and even if they were their erudition would not help them in criticizing Greek and Latin books. "Scholastic discussion is a pleasant little game for scholars to play among themselves, but not to be confused with history"—which apparently, is a superior subject mere scholars have nothing to do with.

What then are we to substitute for scholarship? Mr. Rascoe answers in no uncertain terms—there is nothing about which Mr. Rascoe is ever uncertain. Common sense, unimpaired by special knowledge, in its state of nature, pure and undefiled. Practical good sense can free men from the necessity of toiling over Greek and Latin texts: "To say that the origin of Greek dramas like the *Medea* was in dithyrambic songs and dances sounds as absurd to me as to say the origin of *Man and Superman* was the cancan." And so dismiss the dithyramb. Why bother about a thing that sounds absurd? Or again: "Most modern scholars scoff at this account, but I see no reason for not accepting it as being probably in essentials, true." These are the intuitive convictions arrived at by the unhampered use of sturdy common sense. It is the perfect method for a busy democracy. Both swift acquisition and unquestioning conviction are assured by it. So Mr. Rascoe is enabled to get in very rapid work. Along with the dithyramb, he disposes summarily of the heretofore unanimous belief that Greek tragedy has a religious element. "It is the very reverse of religious." Then the way the Greek alphabet is pronounced is declared to be a monument to the scholars' prejudices and the right way is indicated—all in a paragraph. In a few words he solves the Homeric question, "which has some-how unaccountably puzzled and confused Greek scholars;" and the anthropologists are succinctly corrected in their ideas about how hero worship and religious cults arise. The economists he does not trouble to refute in detail. They are all so wrong about the Trojan War that with a simple "Bosh to them" he turns his back upon them. It is the Declaration of Independence restated: all men are born free and equal and every man is to be his own scholar.

Not only is the scholarly method thus proved completely fallacious, but the scholars are shown to be false pretenders, ignorant of the very Greek and Latin books they have claimed to spend their lives studying—Professor Zimmern, for instance. He is supposed to be an authority on how the Greeks lived, but he does not even know what the Greeks themselves said their houses were like. The reason for his errors, Mr. Rascoe points out, is that he does not know Homer. If he will just read the *Iliad,* he can learn as much on this point as Mr. Rascoe himself knows. Professor Murray's case, however, is a good deal worse. Indeed of all the scholastic breed he is the most conspicuously wrong. To be sure, in one point Mr. Rascoe discusses, "he is not unique in this error; all the other commentators I have read share it," but that fact does not help him with Mr. Rascoe. "Such scholars have got the cart before the horse," he ex-plains—a procedure perfectly in keeping with their gen-eral muddlement. Mr. Rascoe gives what help he can. He advises Professor Murray to read more Greek, at any rate as much as Mr. Rascoe has been able to achieve—along with all of literature up to our present time. "If Professor Murray had read Hippocrates," he would have understood the real force of a—supposedly—familiar Greek suffix just as well as Mr. Rascoe does. And if he had put a little more thought into his lifelong study of Euripides, "he would understand these plays. He would realize that Euripides was a very daring innovator in dramatic technique, language, and point of view." This is as scathing an indictment of scholarly ineptitude as could be made, for it convicts Professor Murray of the darkest scholastic crime, impenetrable ignorance. He actually does not know that Aristophanes in the *Frogs*, although he himself translated it, declares Euripides to be an innovator—in complete agreement with Mr. Rascoe. Surely after this the scholar is to be dismissed from our consideration.

And yet one very troublesome claim of scholars remains to be disposed of: they say they can read Greek easily. This, if true, would constitute a real claim to special privilege. But Mr. Rascoe demolishes it. He has a dark suspicion of general untrustworthiness on the part of anyone who declares he can read well a foreign tongue, but it reaches complete scepticism if that tongue is ancient Greek. Of course, the reason is clear. The idea of reading Greek easily is completely undemocratic. It is based upon the supposition that there are things the everyday man cannot do and, still worse, it suggests that the people who read it best can best judge it. So it is ruled out. It is false: Mr. Rascoe does not believe that anyone can read Greek with ease.

Oddly enough, he concentrates his attack upon those who claim to be able to read Sophocles. I confess this puzzles me. I should have thought other writers would be better examples of difficult Greek, Pindar, for instance, or Aeschylus in all of his plays except the *Prometheus*. But Mr. Rascoe has clearly suffered from Sophocles, and it is he he uses to lash the scholars with: "Whatever any Greek scholar may say to the contrary, Sophocles presents enormous difficulties when one tries to read him in the original." The scholar who claims to be able to understand him is simply telling lies. The truth is, Sophocles is so "excessively literary (*sic*) that we do not know what whole sentences and strophes in his text mean. We can only guess at them." And so he has become the scholars' delight, "A special pet and bugaboo with which to frighten the unscholarly." But no more. This malign power is now ended: "Whenever anybody writes about the superior enjoyment of reading Sophocles in the original because the poetry of Sophocles cannot be rendered into English that person is a humbug." Exit Sophocles along with all the hypocritical scholars who down through the ages have cheated a credulous world into believing they really could read Greek.

Still another method of approach is necessitated by the democratic principle. In a democracy of free and independent citizens each man is to be his own standard. To look higher than one's own level would be a tacit admission of aristocracy. Mr. Rascoe measures all things by himself. What he does not understand—if there is such a thing—is negligible; what he most admires is most admirable. He is completely sincere in this conviction. He has never had an idea that there could be anything beyond him. Perhaps the most striking example of this attitude is what he says about tragedy. To him that strange transmutation of pain into exaltation, which some of the world's greatest minds have puzzled over, is a perfectly simple and not very important matter: "After they had all had a good cry they felt better. That is all there is to Aristotle's famous doctrine of the 'purging of the emotions of pity and terror' by means of tragedy." For Mr. Rascoe never felt anything more than that when he saw *Lear* or *Hamlet*—never any exaltation touched him or glimpse of high passion awed him. Awe, of course, is a glimpse of incomprehensibles, and nothing is incomprehensible to Mr. Rascoe. And so that is all there is to tragedy—just a good cry.

Thus does Mr. Rascoe lay a broad and straight and well macadamized road through the great forest of knowledge, heretofore traversed only by circuitous ways where the question mark, abhorred of Mr. Rascoe, abounded, and the end was often a dark thicket of uncertainties now proved to be completely nonexistent.

There is in an old medieval manuscript, a catechism for the use of young aspirants to scholarship, which begins thus:

"What is a scholar?

"It is a man learning things excellent with assiduous care.

"Of what substance is the scholar?

"A substance endowed with the higher powers of the mind and sensitive, susceptible to learning and to excellence."

But of course Mr. Rascoe would tell me that this description is probably a mere pretension and is certainly completely dated.

THESE
SAD YOUNG MEN

❧❧❧

Published in "The Atlantic Monthly," May, 1929

1

"We have come, willy-nilly, to see the soul of man as commonplace and its emotions as mean. . . . The death of Tragedy is, like the death of Love, one of those emotional fatalities as the result of which the human as distinguished from the natural world grows more and more a desert."

So Mr. Joseph Wood Krutch in a recent number of the *Atlantic.* He is by no means a lonely voice crying in the wilderness of this desert world. Quite a number of young people are with him. A perusal of their writings almost persuades one that, however it may be with Tragedy and Love, laughter is in imminent peril. Mr. Aldous Huxley, for instance:

I'm so tired of all the rubbish about the higher life and moral and intellectual progress and living for ideals and all the rest of it. It all leads to death. Christians and moralists and cultured aesthetes and bright young scientists—all the poor little human frogs, just going pop, ceasing to be anything but the fragments of a little frog—decaying fragments at that. The whole thing's a huge stupidity, a huge disgusting lie.

Life could have been so beautiful . . . Yes, and it *was* beautiful once. Now it is just an insanity; it's just death violently galvanized, twitching about and making a hellish hullaballoo to persuade itself that it isn't really death. . . . Think of New York.

To multiply quotations would be to incur the danger of monotony—a danger, it may be noted, which these young writers themselves do not shrink from. Their denunciations —I beg their pardon. They would not do anything so unsophisticated as to denounce; they would be faintly, ironically, amused at being supposed to care enough about anything to denounce it. Let me say, then, that their gestures of futility are all singularly alike. They are in complete agreement that most things worth while died the day before yesterday and that by the day after tomorrow none will be left. Love, for instance—the love of man and woman —is no more, Mr. Krutch tells us. Once it was potent, in Victorian times even especially so. In the 1890's few escaped its illusion. But no more. We see it clearly now as mere bathos or an obscene joke. "In the general wreck, the wreck of love is conspicuous." Portentous times, these of ours, which in a decade or two completely finished off what has been a mainspring of human action ever since men first started writing books. "Vertiginous rapidity," comments Mr. Krutch, and on this point he will command a universal agreement. Anything, it would appear, in Mr. Krutch's world, may happen overnight.

A by-product of the works of these despondent young

people, which may well prove in the end their most important contribution, is to give a new vantage point to those who uphold the value of a classical education. For the classical student learns inevitably to see human nature and human life, in the broad outline, as a fairly invariable constant. It is impossible for one rooted and grounded in the classics to feel the uniqueness of the present. How often when the dangerous youth of today are being arraigned by despairing elders I have thought of Aristophanes or Xenophon or Isocrates yearning for "the good old kind of education," the days, now past forever, alas! when "children were seen, not heard," when "at meals they were not allowed to grab at the dainties and giggle and cross their feet," when "young people were courteous to their elders and honored their parents," when boys "were an impersonation of modesty—instead of running after ballet-girls." Now, all lament, the children are tyrants in their families and hardly better in their schools. Alcibiades boxed the ears of his literature teacher! What is the world coming to!

That question is echoed by generation after generation. This terrible new world that our fathers knew not of—what will become of it?

> *Hora novissima, tempora pessima sunt,*
> *vigilemus!*

cried Bernard of Cluny in the twelfth century—a strange new day, a time the very worst that there could be. And, as every schoolboy knows, Cicero is credibly reported to have exclaimed, "*O tempora! O mores!*" Never an age that is not appalled at its own depravity.

2

The point is one I should like to urge on all these sad young men. The thing that hath been is that which shall be, and there is no new thing under the sun. Let the young writers take heart. From any point of view of the past it would appear something more than a possibility that the end of all good things is not yet in sight. Indeed, the classical student is so far from the vision of mankind slipping swiftly down a steep decline that he is apt to find his discouragement in what appears to him the patent fact that through the millenniums and the cataclysms of history the human heart remains so astoundingly the same. Within that inner world a thousand years are but as yesterday when it is past; the joys and griefs, the hopes and fear, of Aristophanes' Athenians are ours today.

Mr. Huxley, Mr. Krutch, and the rest, ultramoderns as they conceive themselves to be, are yet not a new product. They have been known before. Nor are they the veritable moderns. It is true that that which we call the modern mind is also not the product of today. As I have said elsewhere, its exponents exist in every age and every generation. When Professor Murray made Euripides popular in the first years of this century, people read him with amazement that he was so modern. Today those to whom the ways of 1900 are hopelessly dated still find themselves astonishingly at home in him. In 400 B.C. they felt in the same way, and when old age shall this generation waste, Euripides will remain, still speaking to those who are in the vanguard of their time. He is the outstanding exponent of the modern mind. The young writers under consideration have nothing

in common with him. Those who possess the modern mind
are the people who never feel pain commonplace or suffering trivial. They are peculiarly sensitized to "the giant
agony of the world." What they see as needless misery
around them and what they envisage as needless misery to
come are intolerable to them. Mr. H. G. Wells cannot
sleep at night for thinking of what will happen to England
when the coal age is over; he feels a very passion of despairing grief.

To such men it is past bearing to wait for the slow and
clumsy adjustments in the passing of years and centuries
of time: to look on helplessly while mankind takes what
is so clearly the wrong turning or fails to take what is so
manifestly the right. The world to them is made up of individuals, each with a terrible power to suffer, and the
poignant pity of their own hearts precludes them from any
philosophy in the face of this awful sum of pain, and any
capacity to detach themselves from it. "We grope for the
wall like the blind . . . we stumble at noon day as in the
night; we are in desolate places as dead men. . . . We look
for judgment, but there is none; for salvation, but it is
far off from us. . . . And justice standeth afar off: for
truth is fallen in the street, and equity cannot enter. Yea,
truth faileth. . . . We are all as an unclean thing . . . and
we all do fade as a leaf." Seven hundred years before Christ
those words were written by the greatest modern mind of
Judaea. Such men must bear the burden of the valley of
vision, but that vision and that protest are not thrown
away. "The life without criticism," Plato says, "is not
worthy to be lived." The possessors of the modern mind
are the perpetual critics, and, whatever else they fail to
shatter, complacent self-content shrivels before them.

Side by side with this profoundly serious spirit there exists another which has superficial points of resemblance but is in reality completely different—the spirit that animates our despairing young writers. The modern spirit has its roots in pain; it suffers for mankind. Quite the reverse is true of the other. It is Byronic; its despair is not the result of suffering, but the source of gratification. I venture the assertion that no one who is not young and fortunate is capable of it. A pleasing self-consciousness is a foremost feature. Alone, high above the thoughtless herd, stands the disillusioned youth, completely aware of its sad eminence. So Lara when our grandfathers were young:

> A vital scorn of all,
> As if the worst had fall'n which could befall.

So Manfred and Childe Harold:

> If it be life to wear within myself
> This barrenness of spirit and to be
> My own soul's sepulchre—
> We are alike unfit
> To sink or soar. . . . We breathe
> The breath of degradation.

So too Mr. Krutch:

Distrusting its thought, despising its passions, realizing its impotent unimportance in the universe, it [our society today] can tell itself no stories except those which make it still more acutely aware of its trivial miseries.

The idiom changes and the outward semblance. Marble brows and clustering curls of raven hue and gloomy grace and all that chilling mystery of mien are gone. Undoubtedly we have lost in picturesqueness. We have exchanged the Hellespont for the subway. But the spirit is unchanged and we need not weep for the Hellespont. Beyond all question some future generation will be lamenting the lost beauty of the alternations of light and gloom, the jeweled ruby and emerald lights against the blackness, the sense of rushing through the unseen, once enjoyed in the ancient subway. The setting passes, but that is all.

Mr. Aldous Huxley's Byronism is not quite of this order. In the nineties Wilde was the most distinguished exponent of the Byronic spirit, and Mr. Huxley inclines that way rather than to the simpler, older form. The paradox enchants him just as it did Wilde. "One way of knowing God," Mr. Huxley's foremost character in *Point Counter Point* concludes, "is to deny him." That is Wilde to the echo. Paradox after paradox used to flow from him: not to pray was more devotional than to pray; ignorance of oneself to be preferred to knowledge; the artist perfect in proportion as he produced nothing, and so on and so on. Mr. Huxley can match them all, the only difference being that Wilde merely talked, and Mr. Huxley, appropriately to the age he lives in, uses a loud speaker: "Telling men to obey Jesus literally is telling them to behave like idiots and finally like devils"; "Your little stink-pot of a St. Francis . . . only succeeding in killing whatever sense or decency there was in him—the disgusting little pervert"; "Deaf and purblind, the outward and visible sign of inward and spiritual truth"; "The real charm of the intellectual life is its easiness. . . . The intellectual life is child's play, which is why intellectuals tend to become children, and then imbeciles, and finally homicidal lunatics and wild beasts." Again quotation becomes monotonous. The recipe is too apparent: take anything men agree is true and state the exact opposite. That, one would suppose, would be revealed to Mr. Huxley as even easier than the intellectual life. The underlying motive is, in his case just as in Wilde's, to assert the sense of superiority which is essential to Byronism. To startle and not be startled—all the naïve egotism of youth is in that desire.

3

But there are many examples of the spirit Byron has forever stamped. Mr. Ernest Hemingway harks back to yet another model. It seems a far cry from *La Dame aux Camélias* to *The Sun Also Rises*, but, for all the outward difference, Mr. Hemingway and Dumas *fils* are brothers under the skin. When the lady with the camellias renounces forever the love of her life, in that moment of excruciating agony her active consciousness leaves her. What she does she knows not, but her unconscious self is guided by the exalted determination of her sacrifice, and in the morning she wakes up in the bed of the marquis—or was it the duke? Another man, at all events. This is the great moment that reveals the sheer nobility of her heroic denunciation. In Mr. Hemingway's novel the sex is changed, but that is all: the hero in his great moment is the reincarnation of the fair, frail lady. In a Spanish cabaret he sits with the girl of his adoration. Enters a magnificent young toreador to whom the lady succumbs instantly. She tells the hero that she must have him and that he, who loves her so madly, must get him for her. No less than Dumas' heroine does he show the heights that true love can rise to. He goes

up to the superb young Spaniard; he tells him his errand
in clear, unfaltering accents; back to her side he brings
him; he feels the repercussion of two passions meeting; and
past the sneering crowd, who realize the full significance
of his act, he walks out—alone—into the blackness of the
night. The idiom, of course, shows marked variations from
type. *La dame* and her Armand converse in terms of high-
flown rhetoric, while Mr. Hemingway's hero and heroine
bid each other go to hell with unvarying persistency, but
the informing spirit changes not at all. It is hardly necessary to point out that the heroine of Mr. Michael Arlen's
best-known novel is also of this order. The end of the lady
with the green hat will occur to everyone as a very slight
variation on Dumas' theme.

Dumas *fils* we know by now to be an arrant sentimen-
talist. It is so easy to recognize sentimentality in the dress
of another age: a haughty young figure posed against Greek
columns; a mantle flung over one shoulder; a proudly curl-
ing lip; an air of weary disdain. We smile appreciatively.
But to see it as clearly in the dress of our own day, in the
very most modish and up-to-date costume—that is another
matter. These hard-headed, ultramodern young people, who
seemed so far removed from any least touch of sentimentality? They are not; their world-weary sophistication differs
in no essential from Byron's or from his prototypes' through
the ages. Each generation of the young looks with amused
or lofty superiority at its fond and foolish elders, and pro-
claims itself the finally disillusioned; and each is as sentimental as it is the prerogative of youth forever to be.

Sentimentality is a most curious thing. Nothing else
assumes so many cunning disguises; nothing is harder to
define. To assert, however, that it is based on unreality is

to venture on no debatable ground; so much is of common consent. By it we escape from the tyranny of fact. Only a very few, the true *âmes d'élite*, are completely free from it by nature; the rest of us must trust to the faulty and fickle education of circumstance. It used to be considered the peculiar prerogative of women, but the reason was only that they were sheltered in large measure from the world of fact. Women were not sentimental about their own facts; they were not often enthusiastic about dishwashing and child-bearing. When they talked as if they were, it was because they found it wise policy to echo the unbounded enthusiasm men have always had for these pursuits. It was when the women ventured beyond their own experience that they became sentimental. Experience is the only corrective; to go beyond what one has oneself felt is to become infallibly and inevitably sentimental. Sincerity and sentimentality are incompatible; sentimentality is unconscious insincerity. And the one and only basis of sincerity is that most difficult page in the book of human knowledge, self-knowledge, the power to distinguish between what one has experienced and what one has not.

Mr. Aldous Huxley and his kind are sentimental because they write of what they have not felt. They do not, certainly as yet, belong to the rank of those who can completely transcend the limitations of their own experience, and they have turned aside from the difficult task of seeking within themselves what they know for themselves is the truth indeed. When Shakespeare says in words the most terrible ever spoken of human life that

It is a tale
Told by an idiot, full of sound and fury,
Signifying nothing,

we bear it; we catch a glimpse of a depth of pain that awes us. Before that mystery of suffering, protest is silenced. When Mr. Huxley or Mr. Krutch tells us that humanity is contemptible and life a trivial misery that has no meaning, we can afford to smile. Whoever finds pain trivial, whoever lightly despises human life, is still living on the surface. He has not yet had "the great initiation," which alone entitles him to touch upon great themes.

> None can usurp this height . . .
> But those to whom the miseries of the world
> Are misery, and will not let them rest.

Like the nineteenth-century women who talked in tones of shocked purity about the horrid world of politics, these young men have gone beyond the field of their experience. Clever young men, brilliant young men—the pity, we feel, that they who undoubtedly know much that we ordinary mortals are cut off from do not confine themselves to cultivating their own garden and wait awhile before trying to compass the boundless horizon. The world is a very big and a very surprising place; human beings are forever acting in incalculable ways. To comprehend the soul, Plato tells us, we have to understand the whole of nature—no light matter. Our young writers would do well to consider Sir Thomas Browne: "Think of things long past and long to come, acquaint thyself with the Choragium of the Stars, and consider the vast expansion beyond them. *Have a glimpse of incomprehensibles.*" The best receipt for shrinking the world to the dimensions of one's own garden is to measure it by oneself.

Mr. Aldous Huxley is a witty raconteur, with a keen eye

for the ironies of life. We could enjoy him as a kind of twentieth-century Jane Austen if he would only leave the universe alone and learn to laugh at himself. What should we not have lost if Miss Austen had been unable to laugh, if she had persisted in holding up Mr. Collins to damn the Christian Church, and Mr. Wickham to damn all the rest? Schnitzler's Anatol and Max can match any of Mr. Hemingway's bad young men, but Schnitzler takes them for what they are, not as an argument of despair for mankind. In that book of balance and proportion, *Gentlemen Prefer Blondes*, Miss Anita Loos does not bring an indictment against the universe in the person of Lorelei. She knows how to laugh, and that knowledge is the very best preservative there is against losing the true perspective. Let the young men beware. Without a sense of humor one must keep hands off the universe unless one is prepared to be oneself an unconscious addition to the sum of the ridiculous.

4

Modern life—that is what this disillusioned generation feels to be intolerable. The Age of Man's Domination by Machines. From the terror of it Mr. Huxley looks back longingly to the Bronze Age. Unfortunately there are so few records of what happened then, but one cannot but conceive some of the features of it as alarming; and involuntarily one is set to wondering what Mr. Huxley would do confronted with a sabre-toothed tiger, when he cannot face a victrola and can hardly endure a motor car. Mr. Krutch is less drastic in his historic preferences. The Age of Pericles for him, or of Elizabeth, when gorgeous Tragedy was still alive. But if Mr. Krutch would ponder certain parts of

Shakespeare and re-read all of Aristophanes, he might be convinced that other things too were then alive even less desirable than modern Gnosticism.

That "paralysis of the will by the intellect" which Mr. Krutch so deplores, as Stendhal did a hundred years before him, has always been the peculiar distinction of the little —very little—band of those who in each age are completely conscious of being the intelligentsia. No generalization based upon them about life in the past or life now can be valid. One fact would seem beyond dispute: modern life does not furnish a soft berth for a weak will. Undoubtedly man in the past had to bear discomforts far beyond any known today, but the patient endurance of misery has never ranked high among those qualities that make us men. Life today demands not less effort than life once did, but more. A peasant ploughing his furrow becomes a workman on the girders of a skyscraper catching red-hot rivets flung at him through space. The engineer on a continental express must have qualities Mr. Weller aloft on his stagecoach was never called upon to exercise. To be sure, Mr. Krutch's point of view is not unique; undoubtedly when the first man hoisted a bit of bark to sail his boat across the river without aid from him, those watching on the bank despaired for the future of mankind now that manly vigor was no more to be exercised. But as yet electricity and steam heat and telephones have not played a determining part in shaping human character. Life in a great modern city still makes its own urgent demands for hard living. Here is not the place, nor is mine the power, to sing the Age of Industrialism. That will be done when another era has dawned, by some *laudator temporis acti*. The point I would press is that—strange mystery of human nature—we refuse ever to take our ease. If it were not so, if with each time-saving and space-shortening device the effort put into life lessened, we should be well in sight by now of the end of the downward path, Capuans warranted to make any Hannibal effeminate. But as soon as one world is conquered we must have another instantly to essay. When we are not obliged to live dangerously we choose to do so. Our attention not being engaged by Indians trying to tomahawk us, we turn it of our own free will to making airplanes. No less than in the days of old are we driven on by the adamantine goddess, stern Necessity. Only her form has changed.

The enfeeblement of the spirit of man, which has already brought us to a point where we cannot find either love or nobility any more in the world—this is Mr. Krutch's central thesis. The spirit of man, which nothing in the past was ever able to subdue, is fallen and will never rise again. I would that our young men could be persuaded to add to their litany one more petition: from swift and shallow generalization, good Lord, deliver us. Eyes as keen as Mr. Krutch's undoubtedly are—if he would but take time to commune with his own heart, and be still—are not needed to discern today the shining spirit of the gay adventurer rejoicing to risk all. That which moved Sir Richard Grenville sailing the little *Revenge* against the Spanish Armada is one with Lindbergh in the spaces over the sea. The Crusaders aflame for the Holy City become the doctors who die to discover the cause of a disease. Heroism in its two distinctive forms so clearly here beside us. And, even more to give us courage for what is to come, an ever-rising tide of human kindness, a deepening conviction that we are, in most practical fact, our brother's keeper, due not to any essential difference in the spirit, but to the fact that the focus has shifted. It has moved away from the single man, king, hero, saint, raised on high for all to see, to the indistinguishable units that make up the hurrying crowds, to the anonymous individual. No longer the general, but the regiment; not the captain any more than the crew; not this or that great single figure, but the nameless heroes, the engineers, the bridge builders, the workers in steel and steam and electricity and dynamos and turbines and all the things that build and drive this mighty age. We are asserting in our own terms what every age in its own way has voiced, the profoundest conviction of humanity—the worth of human life. In truth, if we do not allow ourselves to grow impatient with the vagaries of adolescent thought which are, after all, so natural, we can perceive in the very restlessness and bewildered unhappiness of many of our young people a sign of that strangest of all the strange things that move within us, "the mysterious preference for the best." "He who finds it miserable not to be a king, must be a king dethroned"—the consciousness of our finiteness, of our insignificance, of our misery, is the seal of our greatness.

PRIVATE IDIOM

❦

The two great dominant intellectual influences today are Einstein and Freud. Einstein has introduced us to a new universe where clear certainty, once the happy prerogative of the scientists, is fading away into a region not strictly determined by cause and effect, not amenable to exact interpretation. Freud has turned us from the brightly lit world without, to the dimly discerned world within. The result of the impact of the two has been to throw us into a state of confusion.

In all the past I do not know of any change in the mental and spiritual atmosphere comparable with that to which we have to adjust ourselves. After all, there was no real break between Greece and Rome. Cicero could have passed quite well for a Greek—at a Roman dinner party—and Plutarch seems to have been very much at home in Rome. The Renaissance was only a discovery of the past which had never completely vanished from men's minds. The Reformation was primarily a rediscovery of the individual whom Greece had discovered long before. And although the ordeal was severe when the Church came up against the *Origin of Species*, that was a long, slow battle. The general point of view changed almost imperceptibly. But we ourselves within a few years have become fully aware that our world is a new and strange place. We are facing two new universes, and we do not know the laws that govern either.

Our ancient inheritance of the ages seems to have little significance in helping us, the difference is so great between our point of view and that of the generations before us. The past was always dependent on authority except for a brief time in Greece, and today authority has ceased to be authoritative. The change appears most clearly in science where the battle between the scientists and the Church authorities was fierce and long-drawn-out and the effort to keep the mind within theological walls was conspicuously defeated. In art the change came much later, but by now the artists too have definitely rejected their authorities, not merely the old conventions that a Madonna must be painted in a blue dress and the like, but the authority of the great masters of the past, who were authoritative because they were revered, and followed so that a human face, for instance, was painted on the general lines they had worked along, to resemble a real face. The same is true of religion. There, too, authority has grown weak, or, more accurately, the inner is becoming authoritative at the expense of the outer.

The search for God is coming forward as the business of religion, and the use of God as a means to safety is receding. More and more we see that the reward of the pure in heart is that they shall see God, not that they shall be saved, as the Westminster catechism puts it, from the pains of hell forever. Religion is no longer an indestructible bank into which we can put our savings and receive a good return. It is taking on the aspect of a spiritual venture. We are thinking less along the lines of "The Lord shall make thee plenteous in goods, to bless all the works of thine hand," and more of Him who "satisfieth the longing soul and filleth the hungry soul with goodness." The inner is gaining over the outer. Not an outside infallible Church, or an outside infallible Book, but that which is within, "the true Light that lighteth every man coming into the world."

Religion is not losing out in Freud's universe any more than science is losing out in Einstein's. It has nothing ultimately to fear from any method of probing the human soul, for it is founded upon men's deepest need, the need for God, and upon God's answer to that need.

But how is it with art, the third great department of the human spirit? What do we see there today? Freud's influence, all powerful. Art is first of all selection. Consider the art of writing. The writer's basic material, his tool, so to speak, is *Webster's Unabridged*. He has to select from that, from the vast number of words, his own significant words, and he has to select his subject from all that the wide world offers. Art is based on the selection of the significant. But selection is directly opposed to Freud. Everything is significant to him. No detail is unimportant. Do you dream of a railroad, two strips of metal bare and unadorned? It has a vital meaning. Do you dream of it twice? It becomes more vital. Repetition is illuminating and revealing. Each time you repeat yourself you gain in significance.

How these fundamental Freudian ideas have influenced the writers is apparent to the most casual reader, especially how they have seized upon them when treating Freud's dominant motif, sex. The long, long novels our authors, the very best of them, go on producing, full of endless details, all presented as equally important, full of endless scenes with one woman and another and yet another, all following exactly the same procedure—I have never read one without recalling Horace's advice to young writers, that when they reach their final draft, "Be sure that more is cut out than is left in."

Art and Freud are at odds, and it is not hard to see which is coming off best. Our artists, our painters, musicians, poets, are self-engrossed as never before. They are exploring Freud's universe, and the world outside is unimportant. On the last page of *Look Homeward, Angel* when the hero "saw in his moment of terrible vision his foiled quest of himself, he stood naked and alone in darkness; he stood upon the ramparts of his soul, before the lost land of himself; heard inland murmurs of lost seas. 'O sudden and impalpable faun, lost in the thickets of myself, I will hunt you down. I heard your footfalls in the desert; I saw your shadow in old buried cities, but I did not find you there. But in the city of myself, upon the continent of my soul, I shall find a door where I may enter.' "

The passage illustrates to perfection the Freudian artist's self-absorption. Wolfe was a fairly early explorer of Freud's universe, but in that respect no one as yet has gone farther in it. Long before Freud there were restless, wretched seekers in literature, but they did not do their seeking in the lost land of themselves. Tolstoy's Levin and Pierre followed a quest as exacting as that of Wolfe's hero. They suffered agonies of frustration and despair equal to his, but they had to find the answers to their questionings in something greater than themselves. Both found it in God. To Levin the clue was goodness; to Pierre it was seeing the infinite and eternal in everything. Wolfe does not tell us if his Eugene ever found his answer. He abandons him just as he starts on that determined search into the thickets of himself. It is inconceivable that Wolfe would have done so if he had discovered his own solution as Tolstoy did. Wolfe's exploration did not lead him to the door where he could enter, and that is true so far of all the Freudian writers.

Style and method of writing have suffered as great a change, perhaps greater. The old *lingua franca*, which artists the world over spoke and their audiences everywhere understood, has almost disappeared. An artist speaks in his own private language, not caring if it is unintelligible to the people who look at pictures or listen to music or read books. I do not mean Joyce or Gertrude Stein. I knew Gertrude Stein, and I once told her that I thought I understood how she wrote because occasionally just as I was falling asleep I would have a feeling as if a cog had slipped in my brain and a flood of disconnected words would flow effortlessly through my mind, sometimes in the most amusing sequences. I may say that it never occurred to me to write them down for other people's consideration. She told me that was just what happened to her, except that she was able to turn the cog off and on at will. But however good an example she was of the stream of consciousness, she was imperfectly Freudian. When she had something she wanted to say, as in the autobiography or her experience with American soldiers in France, she wrote simply and intelligibly. There is nothing in those books like "Toasted Suzy is my ice cream," which she told me was the best line she had ever written.

Exactly the same is true of Joyce. In *A Portrait of the Artist as a Young Man* there is not one incomprehensible sentence. He had something he wished to convey to other people and he did so in plain English. I am not speaking of deliberate unintelligibility, which will never be taken seriously in the long run, but of the very serious fact that the clarity of art is departing in this new universe of self-knowledge Freud has opened to us.

Michelangelo did not regard his work as that of knowing himself and being forced by the depth of his knowledge to express it in terms few people if any could understand. He wanted to set forth what he saw as outside of himself and do it so clearly that all could catch at least a glimpse of it. His lofty task was in part to banish obscurities and perplexities for them and make them share in his vision. He clarified the truth of beauty and the beauty of truth so that people saw them where they never had before.

Years ago when I was in Paris, there was an exhibition of cubist paintings, one of the very first, if not the first of all. I was curious about the work of these new men, and I went to see it. I found myself in a room where the walls were covered with canvases full of brown and tan planes, nothing but that, planes inclining in different directions, all of them in various shades of brown. The only person there except myself was a man who stood in deep absorption before one of them. I watched him a long time and he never moved. Finally I ventured to go up to him and say, "You find it beautiful?" "Very beautiful," he said in a deep voice. "I am an artist in Brussels. I have come here just to see this exhibition." We both contemplated the canvas in silence. Then he said quickly and excitedly, "It is a portrait. I am sure it is. See, here is a button, and down lower —there—I have just found another. Certainly it is the portrait of a man." I left him to his voyage of discovery. It was the first time I had come up against artists using a method of expression that could be understood only after long study, if at all.

The other day I told a distinguished young poet, who had lately won a notable prize, that the only line of strictly modern poetry I knew by heart was, "We are the eyelids of defeated caves." He said, "I know the man who wrote that." "Then," I said hopefully, "you can tell me what it means." He meditated. "No," he said, "I cannot. But when I see him I will ask him."

Keats said, "All great poetry should produce the instantaneous conviction, 'This is true.'"

The cult of the incomprehensible, in music, in painting, and in poetry, is spreading and our loss is immeasurable. Those who are struggling to explore and express for us the new universe within, which is so strange to us, sometimes gifted souls who in other ages would have been our seers and interpreters, do not speak to us in a way we can understand. Often it seems that they do not care to, that they are content to be understood only by themselves. So we are losing in this distracted world the illumination of art given by our own contemporaries, spoken by those who live in the same atmosphere with us, the beauty and the elevation and the interpretation of the mystery which artists in other days were able to express to their contemporaries.

The incomprehensible in literature is not peculiar to our times. It had charms for writers long before the modern world began. What resulted then is worth considering. In the old story of Antaeus, Hercules could not kill the giant as long as he was in contact with the earth. If he so much as touched it, power flowed into him, but when Hercules held him up in the air he was easily killed. History shows that when a literature floats away from the solid ground of the common speech to a language peculiar to itself, when it disdains the public stage and seeks only a small private audience, it is nearing its end. As the gap widens between the way people talk and the way people write, what is born is a thing called closet literature, quite properly. If it stays shut up in the closet it perishes for lack of air.

In Latin, as the close of a great literature drew near, writers began to regard words not as means to express thoughts, but as an end in themselves, words for the sake of words. More and more the idea of writing became divorced from the idea of communication, of sharing with others what was in the writer's mind. Finally poems, so called, were composed only to please the eye. Written down in lines of varying lengths they took on the shape of some pleasing object, an hourglass, a vase, a shepherd's pipe. The content had no importance. Why be captious and seek for a meaning in an arrangement of the alphabet so agreeable to look at? No one to date has gone as far along that particular path as the Latins did, but there are indications that we are headed that way.

But however the approach varies from one age to another, the result is always the same, unintelligibility. I was being shown through the enormous examination halls in Nanking where only a few decades ago passing an examination had raised the butcher's and the baker's sons to the rank of noblemen. My guide, an intelligent young Chinese, was, he told me, a graduate of the Methodist University there. I asked him, "Which do you value most, the Eastern or the Western learning?" "Oh, the Eastern," he said eagerly. But, I pointed out, the five great classics were very hard to understand and sometimes completely incomprehensible. Of course they were, he said, as if that was a crowning excellence. Then he added in a hushed tone, as if he were speaking of something sacred, "My father knows a man, a very great writer, who can write in a way only one other man in China can understand." We are not there yet, but we are on our way.

A private idiom for an artist? It is impossible. The man who uses it is either not an artist or else he is too bewildered by what he has discovered in the still dim realm of self-knowledge to be able to find words for it. Art, all art, is communication; writing is especially so. People do not write to themselves. They write to say things to other people. Of course the artists must explore the strange world within themselves which Freud has opened to us as never before, but they must not stay there. If they find they cannot express what they have seen except by using a language comprehensible only to themselves, if "defeated" seems to them applicable to caves—which also have eyelids—then, if they are wise, they will take warning from the past and stop writing until they have come out from the thickets of themselves and are interested in looking at a cave.

Self-knowledge is perhaps won most easily in solitude. But any one who wants to write what will endure must leave his attic, come down from his ivory tower, and test his discoveries, his truths, in the only final way, by the universal touchstone of their significance in the outside world.

WORDS,
WORDS, WORDS

Nearly one hundred years ago a novelist and a poet, quite forgotten now but highly esteemed in her own day, whose name was Jean Ingelow, wrote:

> Amorphous masses cooing to a monk;
> Some fine old crusty problems very drunk;
> A pert parabola flirting with a don,
> And two Greek grammars with their war paint on.
> A lame black beetle singing to a fish;
> A squinting planet in a gravy-dish.

There were other lines equally striking which, unfortunately, I have forgotten (the book they appeared in is long since out of print), but the importance of even the few I can quote must be instantly apparent to all those interested in the latest fashion in poetry. The widespread belief that we are observing a new development in poets must be discarded. The essential similarity of this nineteenth-century verse to the most modern school is so striking as to be conclusive.

Many writers today could serve as illustration, but none

better than Dylan Thomas, who, the critics assure us, is the greatest of them all. For instance,

> A claw I question from the mouse's bone,
> The long-tailed stone
> Trap I with coil and sheet,
> Let the soil squeal I am the biting man
> And the velvet dead inch out.

No one can fail to see that Thomas is here using Jean Ingelow's technique. It is true that his skill is inferior to hers. Her combinations are far more arresting. Still, trapping a long-tailed stone with a sheet is undoubtedly in its fundamental conception one with her happier efforts. Soil that squeals belongs clearly to the same order as a parabola that flirts, while velvet—with its connotations of luxurious smoothness and softness—is as far away from the dead we have met in life and literature as a planet is from a gravy dish. Although the two verses were written one hundred years apart, they show the same technique, strongly marked.

Are we then to hail Jean Ingelow as the founder of the modern school? The question is an important one which merits careful examination. Unfortunately, we have only a single verse of her essay into this particular poetical field, but it is so forcefully and so vividly written that many pages could hardly illustrate the method better. It can be briefly stated, being at bottom very simple. It is to bring words together which from every possible point of view have nothing to do with one another. Cooing is perhaps the last thing we would expect from amorphous masses or serenading fish from a lame black beetle, or, as in Thomas' verse, squealing from the soil. In Thomas' work the method is seen in its true importance. He makes use of it constantly: "the whinnying light," "the shameful oak," "the long-legged heart," "the cuddled tree," "the snail-waked world," "the heart-shaped voice of the water's dust," "the halfmoon's vegetable eye." Examples can be found in everything he wrote.

> Till every bone in the rushing grave
> Rose and crowed and fell (The crowing bone!)

or

> These stolen bubbles have the bites of snakes
> And the undead eye-teeth

These two quotations show that although their initial start was the same, Thomas has advanced far beyond Jean Ingelow. Her technique is to choose words which will surprise; he aims at a more forceful effect. Bubbles with eye-teeth—and undead ones at that—arouse a livelier emotion than surprise. Also she always makes statements which are easily grasped. When she says that problems are drunk, the meaning—so to speak—is clear, but to Thomas the idea of a meaning is irrelevant, if not to be avoided. The line

> Your calm and cuddled is a scythe of hairs

is typical, so much so that when occasionally he "deviates into sense," the reader is inclined to think that he himself has gone wrong and given profundities a shallow and facile interpretation. But this is rare. For the most part facile interpretations are not possible. As, for instance, in

> Yea the dead stir,
> And this, nor this, is shade,
> the landed crow,

> He lying low with ruin in his ear,
> The cockerel's tide upcasting
> from the fire.

or

> The patchwork halves were cloven as they scudded
> The wild pigs' wood, and slime upon the trees,
> Sucking the dark, kissed on the cyanide,
> And loosed the braiding adders from their hairs;
> Rotating halves are horning as they drill
> The arterial angel.

It would be a rash person who attempted to give a facile interpretation of these verses. There seems little doubt that we shall presently have schools devoted to elucidating Thomas, each championing a view opposed to the others, one of those pleasant literary quarrels which can never be settled.

This is in marked contrast to Jean Ingelow's simple lucidity, but an even greater contrast is underlined by the fact that Thomas' deviations into sense often leave the reader regretful that he has deviated. This time he finds himself thinking, something less than lucidity would be preferable:

> I smell the maggot in my stool.

or

> I sit and watch the worm beneath my nail
> Wearing the quick away.

or

> The redhaired cancer still aline,
> The cataracted eyes that filmed their cloth;
> Some dead undid their bushy jaws,
> And bags of blood let out their flies;

These lines point to the major difference between the two writers, a profound difference. They differ in their spirit. Jean Ingelow can be gay; she amuses herself as well as her readers; she can laugh. It is impossible to conceive of Thomas ever doing so. He is perpetually "not amused." His view of the world is extremely dark. Nature is never his wedding garment, only his shroud. He sees ugliness everywhere. The sea, for example, which poets through the ages have found beautiful and terrible and awe-inspiring and lovely and even laughing (Aeschylus speaks of the "never numbered laughter of sea waves") is to Thomas unpleasant or futile. It is "ramshackling" and "goose-plucked." It has "black, base bones." It is

> The graveyard in the water where
> The crab-backed dead on the sea bed rose
> And scuttled over her eyes.

The sea waves "squawk" or they "sound flowing like blood from the loud wound." He finds the sea generally repulsive. The same is true of Spring, poetry's old favorite. To Thomas she is "bone-breaking"; she "runs angrily"; she "unravels the colic season." He has not a word of praise for her any more than for the sea, unless (it is possible) he means to praise when he writes:

> The spring weather
> That belled and bounded with the fossil

That question cannot be settled here. As much can be said for those who maintain that praise is intended as for those who maintain that it is not. It must be bequeathed to the scholars of the future.

Jean Ingelow clearly has been left far behind. Our conclusion must be that her claim to be founder of modern poetry is based upon method and technique only. The differences between her and Thomas go very deep. Jean Ingelow lived when art was conceived of as lightening the weight of this unintelligible world. The nineteenth-century poets saw their art as bringing clarity into obscurity and order into confusion. They believed that through it they had seen truth, which always banishes obscurity and confusion. The truth of poetry was, they knew, as Aristotle had said, truer than the truth of history. History says Alexander the Great was born in 356 and died in 323. Poetry says,

> Men must endure their going hence,
> even as their coming hither;
> Ripeness is all.

The nineteenth-century poets knew that the actual factual world looked different when the light of poetry was turned on it. Trees without any leaves were actually "bare ruined choirs where late the sweet birds sang." Water was really "the glassy, cool, translucent wave." Old age, always marked out for drab dullness, had in it for the truth of poetry something quite different:

> I am a very foolish, fond old man,
> Fourscore and upward, not an hour more or less,
> And, to deal plainly,
> I fear I am not in my perfect mind.

Whatever of truth these poets saw, they tried to make others see, to show the beauty of truth and the truth of beauty so clearly that those who had never seen them before could catch at least a glimpse.

These ideas are all outmoded. Professor Maritain, the philosopher and the critic and a chief exponent of modern art, says that a distinguishing characteristic of modern poetry is that it has freed itself from "the claims of rational expression" by which classical poetry has always been "repressed." To be sure, he points out, the moderns attach the greatest importance to words, but only in order to "get rid of the language of discursive reason" which "prevents this inner music from being conveyed by the words." "There is an intelligible meaning," he says, "but we don't know what this meaning is."

In brief, Professor Maritain sees the aim of modern poetry as a two-fold method of liberation: "To free itself from nature; to be free from language." "It has an inaudible, wordless, soundless music . . . the music of intuitive pulsions." In it "the logical sense" has been dislocated by the poetic sense, which, he considerately explains to us, is "the inner, ontological entelechy of the poem."

The words open a wide vista. May we look forward to a time when music too will be "free," soundless, and inaudible?

In his look into the trend of modern poetry it almost seems as if the great French critic has failed to see that, with the poetic sense of Joyce and Thomas and a host of others dislocating the logical sense, the future of English poetry can be foretold. There will be a new language for poetry—nay, for every poet. It seems certain that Professor Maritain's exhaustive study of English literature did not lead him to Lewis Carroll or he must have recognized the prophetic importance of

> 'Twas brillig, and the slithy toves
> Did gyre and gimble in the wabe;
> All mimsy were the borogoves,
> And the mome raths outgrabe.

Here there is no trouble about the poetic sense being repressed by the logical sense because there is no sense at all. Carroll has abolished it and pointed out the path for modern poetry. He completed what Jean Ingelow began, and any future history of English literature must give a place of honor to them both.

Many a reader of today's poetry will acclaim such a development when it occurs. We shall no longer have to puzzle, or, much worse, uneasily suspect that there must be something wrong with us, as we do when we are first presented with "benzine rinsings from the moon" or "the scythed boulders bleed." When each poet is his own lexicographer, and poems are made up of words never met before, we shall finally be free to discover an inaudible, wordless, soundless music, the music of intuitive pulsions. Then we can give up trying to fit meanings to words.

WILLIAM FAULKNER

"I detest nature," Picasso has said. He is the spokesman for
the art of the age, our age, for the music we are listening
to, the pictures we are looking at, the books we are reading. Today the usual and the normal, which is to say the
natural, is being discarded. What is called abstract art has
taken a foremost place. One of the most recent prizes was
given to a sculptor for her figure of an animal shape, not
like any animal that ever lived, but a representation of an
indeterminate animal vaguely applicable to many kinds of
living creatures. The sculptor had turned away from nature
to depict an image she had conceived, a form existing only
in her mind. When Picasso detests nature he is doing the
same thing. He shuts out the detestable world his eyes show
him and takes refuge in the inner world of himself where
he perceives shapes only dimly connected with things that
have actual existence.

Our artists are escaping from reality. This is no new
thing, to be sure. In almost all ages there have been artists
who escaped. What is new in our age is the direction they
are taking. In the past a detestation of nature, a determination not to be dominated by fact, led persistently to the
land of heart's desire where everyone and everything was

good and true and beautiful. Now it leads to just the opposite, where nothing is good or true or beautiful. Of course one is just as much an escape as the other. It is just as far from reality to shut out all that is agreeable as to shut out all that is disagreeable. Both extremes are equally unreal, and both are equally romantic.

Romance is the refusal to accept things as they are, "the world being inferior to the soul," as Bacon says. All art bears either the romantic stamp or the classic. To the classic artist his chosen field is things as they are. He is repelled by anything unfamiliar and extraordinary, and he detests extremes. Greek art of course is the pre-eminent example of classic art. The Greeks had no desire whatever to turn away from nature. They did not see the usual and the normal as commonplace. The way they looked at them is perfectly exemplified in the statue of the girl bending over a basin to wash her hands. She is classic art in herself; beauty is embodied in a completely ordinary act. The Greeks saw beauty and significance in nature. If they took a romantic subject like the Iliad, they brought it down to earth and worked it out in ordinary surroundings which to them were not drab and dreary but interesting.

Both trends, the classical and the romantic, have their dangers, which perpetually threaten to destroy them and often have destroyed them. The specter that haunts the classic artist is putting form ahead of spirit, style ahead of matter, polished convention ahead of free realism. The danger to the romantic, equally present whether he turns his back on ugliness or on loveliness, is sentimentality. It is easily recognized in the first case, but not in the second. There is a general impression that to describe things as dull and drab and unpleasant is realism and farthest removed from the roses and raptures of sentimentality. That is not true. The extremely unpleasant can be extremely sentimental. Sentimentality is always false sentiment. It is such a danger to the romantic artist because he has escaped from the domination of fact, and sentimentality is falsehood to fact. When an artist detests nature, he has thrown away his best defence against that danger. Nature is not sentimental. When Edgar Lee Masters describes a baby:

> She was some kind of a crying thing
> One takes in one's arms and all at once
> It slimes your face with its running nose,
> And voids its essence all over you,
> And there you stand smelling to heaven—

he has fallen into one extreme of sentimental unreality as truly as Swinburne has into the other when he writes:

> A baby's eyes—
> Their glance might cast out pain and sin,
> Their speech make dumb the wise,
> By mute glad god-head felt within
> A baby's eyes.

Neither Masters nor Swinburne, of course, were in the least concerned with what a baby is really like. They had escaped from that limitation. Perhaps each in his way was seeking for some other truth than the truth of nature, but all we know is that the result was falsehood for both of them, pure sentimentality, as much in the case of the nasty baby as in the case of the baby with the momentous eyes.

Before the publication of the *Spoon River Anthology* Swinburne's was the prevailing mood. Thereafter the other extreme came into fashion. At present there is a brilliant group devoted to it, and the most brilliant of all is the Nobel Prize winner William Faulkner. He is our leading romanticist today; he too detests nature.

Mr. Faulkner's novels are about ugly people in an ugly land. There is no beauty anywhere. Whether he deliberately excludes it or does not perceive it, no one can say; but at least he says himself that a blossoming pear tree in the moonlight looks like hair streaming up from the head of a drowned woman, each hair distinct in the water from the others. He describes the scent of a blooming shrub, still wet with dew, as sickening. To walk through the woodlands in summer in "a gloom dimmer than the gray desolation of November" is to feel "malicious little eyes" watching (birds? squirrels?) while under foot the oozing earth crawls with snakes.

But the land is worse, far worse, than all of these unpleasant features put together. It ruins the people it nourishes. A dark curse lies on it. It was "already tainted before any white man owned it . . . from that old world's corrupt and worthless twilight as though in the sailfulls of the old world's tainted wind which drove the ships." Columbus', presumably. The initial curse, connected with the dispossession of the Indians, appears to be—Mr. Faulkner is not quite clear about it—inherited by the North as well as the South, but its full effect is shown concentrated in the South. "Don't you see?" young Ike McCaslin cries in "The Bear." "Don't you see? This whole land, the whole South, is cursed, and all of us who derive from it, whom it ever suckled, lie under the curse."

The people, thus doomed, are like the land that dooms them. It is part of the fate that molds them. "Our rivers, our land: opaque, slow, violent, shaping and creating the life of man in its implacable and brooking image." At this point Poe comes irresistibly to mind, "The dank tarn of Auber—the misty mid region of Weir—the ghoul-haunted woodlands of Weir." It is the point in the realm of romance where extremes meet, Poe's lovely and lost Ulalume and Mr. Faulkner's curse-ridden men.

And his women? No one adjective or two can describe them. I confess his attitude to them puzzles me. I know nothing like it in literature outside of *The Golden Bough*. Frazer's account of the way some primitive tribes feel toward young women, the mixture of violent attraction and equally violent repulsion, is just what Mr. Faulkner feels. Young women are not really human to him. He calls them "the Symbol of the ancient and eternal Snake." They are an embodied Menace to Man. Old they are more tolerable, but even in childhood, earliest childhood, they are already initiates of darkly secret rites. "They are born," Mr. Faulkner concludes, "already bored with what a boy approaches only at fourteen or fifteen with blundering and aghast trembling."

There is something familiar back of all this. As I see Mr. Faulkner, he was brought up in a community where religion took the form of condemning most things. Thou shalt not . . . I see him listening as a little boy to accounts of a jealous God, an implacable judge, who punished sin by inflicting suffering, before whose "awful and irrevocable judgement seat"—so he calls it—trembling human beings would have to stand even though they were "predestined," foredoomed to be saved or lost. Most of them to be lost, for humanity was born sinful. The only way to escape inexorable punishment here and hereafter was through the grace of God, mysteriously bestowed upon some, those chosen out for eternal bliss, and as mysteriously withheld from others, those not chosen. A man could not earn this saving grace; he could never deserve it; and yet without it he could not resist the evil which infected him on the day of his birth. Nevertheless, if it was not given him, the fault was his.

These are ideas which have in many periods darkened the world. Children brought up in their shadow will not be apt to see the things that are lovely or many things that are good. In such an atmosphere beauty and enjoyment are suspect, and sex of course is still worse. The relation between the sexes, indeed, always becomes a crucial difficulty. It had to be tolerated. There had to be children, fleshly though their origin was. At this point the Church could be counted on to give a helping hand: marriage was blest of God. Somehow they always made out, but only superficially. All that had to do with the flesh was tainted and all that had to do with sex was the most fleshly and the most tainted of all.

This was a heavy burden to be placed on the shoulders of a little boy who thought about the things he was told. How could a blooming pear tree give him pleasure? Pleasant things were not only futile, they could be a fair cloak hiding what was ugly, and of course the cloak soon ceased to be fair. The eye can be trained not to see. Beauty and all things desirable can vanish out of sight.

Inevitably, gifted as he was, Mr. Faulkner worked his way through this maze of confused instincts and feelings and thoughts. He did it by a logic of his own. People were predestined; that part was true. They did not act of themselves; they were driven. "A volitionless servant of fatality," he calls one of his characters. His own peculiar twist was that they were always predestined to hell. Heaven was non-existent.

So too he had his own way of dealing with the conventional but precarious balancing act, aided and abetted by the Church, between a point where women were spiritually sexless, chastely elevated above the flesh and only yielding to the gross male, and a point where they were shameless sex embodied, tempting man to his fall. That tenuous connection between contradictions he cleared away by the reasonable method of dismissing the first kind of woman, but temperamentally he cannot take to the middle of the road, and so he swept all females together, little girls too. Eves, every one of them, forever holding out the apple to bewildered Adams.

Of course he repudiated the doctrines back of these notions. Mr. Faulkner will not be found in any little church today listening to the imprecatory Psalms. But the ideas of God and man they express molded him and made him what he is. He is to the very depths of him a Puritan, a violently twisted Puritan, a perverted Puritan, and that means something very strange indeed. In *The Sound and the Fury*, Quentin finds out that his sister has been having relations with men. "Have there been very many?" he asks and she answers, "I don't know. Too many," and begs him to look after their father. With that, a plan to help them all leaps into his mind. "I'll tell Father," he says to her, "then it'll have to be because you love Father then we'll have to go away amid the pointing and the horror the clean flame I'll make you say we did you thought it was them but it was me." But, extraordinarily, the idea of incest between his son and daughter is not comforting to father.

In fact he rejects it. He tells Quentin, "i (*sic*) think you are too serious to give me any cause for alarm you wouldn't have felt driven to the expedient of telling me you have committed incest otherwise did you try to make her do it?" Quentin answers No: "i was afraid she might and then it wouldn't have done any good but if i could tell you we did it would have been so and then the others wouldn't be so." The father accepts this as making the matter perfectly clear and tells his son approvingly that he is not lying now. After a little disquisition on the unimportance of everything, he bids Quentin, "go on up to cambridge right away" and "you will remember that for you to go to harvard has been your mother's dream since you were born and no compson [the family name is Compson] has ever disappointed a lady."

Comment seems unnecessary, except perhaps to point out that the passage is notably characteristic of Mr. Faulkner. All that chiefly distinguishes him is there, his stylistic vagaries along with his peculiar brand of Puritanism, his twisted notions of good and bad, and his kinship with the more romantic writers among the earlier Victorians, whose heroes also would never disappoint a lady.

Back of the extremely bleak view he takes of all things here below stands the conviction, older than Puritanism, as old as antiquity, present in all ages, among all nations and races, that there is an inseparable trinity: the world and all that is therein, the flesh and all that are born therefrom, and the devil.

His special gift as a writer—and it is a great gift—is that he can make anything live, no matter how ordinary and trivial, if he chooses to do so. When he takes in hand what he deals with best, a flood, a fire, a storm, he can carry his reader away with him past all damning points of criticism.

Indeed he can do that without any aid from convulsions of nature. In his most popular novel, *Sanctuary*, he is able to sweep on through most improbable events and people and keep up the interest which, in the preposterous circumstances the book spotlights, is an achievement.

Sanctuary, however, was a new experiment for Mr. Faulkner. In his earlier novels, usually considered his best, which were, with one exception, written before that highly colored piece of fiction, he paints a drab, monotonous world. Necessarily so, for there are no contrasts in the picture. There is violence, indeed, and cruelty and all manner of sexual doings, but they merge into the general scene, dimmed like everything else. They are an ugly, insignificant part of what is ugly and without significance. All these books merge with one another. There is the same heavy gray atmosphere, the same undiversified country, the same inconsequent little human beings making the same futile gestures, the writer's art used not to heighten and magnify, but to dull and diminish. Plot, character, the storyteller's tools from Homer on to the latest *Saturday Evening Post* serial, do not interest Mr. Faulkner. How many readers could give a clear account of what happens in any of these novels? Certainly not a single individual in them stands out and is alive. Power of choice, the great individualizer, Mr. Faulkner will not allow them. They are all volitionless servants of fatality, and thereby unimportant, even to their creator.

Wherein his special gift is most brilliantly shown, what he can make come alive most vividly, is an experience—just that, an experience which the reader feels as if it were his own, independent of the person in the book it is attached to, who is there only to give it a locality. There is no feeling necessarily of sympathy with the character or even of understanding him, but only of being oneself put through that suspense, that terror, that remorse.

It is a gift few writers have had. It is especially Mr. Faulkner's for two reasons. First, his characters with few exceptions are not sympathetic or understandable, so that it is easy to detach the emotion from its embodiment as it would not be to detach horror from Raskolnikoff or passion from Anna Karenina. In their case it is what they are feeling that takes possession of us; we have forgotten ourselves. None of Mr. Faulkner's characters have that independent life. The second reason is that he avoids profounder emotions. Love and the suffering bound up with it is not a subject he cares to treat. It is absent even when its presence is urgently required, as in *Requiem for a Nun* where a baby who has been murdered drops out of the picture which has for its center the baby's mother. Her suffering is concentrated on herself; the baby is forgotten.

With the power he has to tell a story, his ability to create tension where he chooses, the storyteller's best gift, he seems deliberately to set up obstacles in the way of his story. His obscurities, his sentences that make no sense, are herein a minor matter. He will never put into comprehensible words anything that is essential to understanding what he wants to get over. But he will keep on interrupting it, breaking it in two. He loves to release a torrent of words that have nothing to do with what has gone before. Suddenly, for no apparent reason, they rush out, tumbling over each other, eddying around the reader like a flood, carrying him this way and that, all sense of direction lost. The feeling of hurry is increased by an absence of capital letters and periods. The impression given is that the writer cannot stop to end a sentence or write a capital. The reader finds himself breathlessly trying to keep up with him while holding on to the story left pages behind. The sense of immediacy, which Mr. Faulkner when he wants can give to anything, has without warning been transferred to some unlikely and irrelevant account of an ancient train of cars, perhaps, or the building of a jail, or the contents of an old ledger—all of them there as if the surge of words, words, words had taken possession of the writer too and was driving him on along with his reader.

These interruptions to the story are much less distressing, of course, when there is nothing of importance to be interrupted. If one is reading a tale told by an idiot, for instance, one does not especially mind being shifted away from the subject, such as it is, to a description of fishing. But in *Intruder in the Dust* there is, surprisingly, a good plot, even an exciting plot—how a boy saves a Negro from being lynched for a murder he did not commit—and there are scenes in it as tense as anything Mr. Faulkner has written. It is infuriating, when one is waiting to see if the boy digging up the murdered man will be quick enough to stop the lynching, to be plunged into long pages describing over and over again what Mr. Faulkner calls accurately "the land fixed in monotonous repetition." One is reduced to wishing that the story could be printed in some special kind of type and the meanderings of Mr. Faulkner's thought in some other kind. Or better still, that he had employed earlier the same technique as in *Requiem for a Nun*. This is a play, and it appears that when Mr. Faulkner comes to the drama, even he cannot stop at a breathless moment to give the history of an old jail, then return to the moment and go on to another crisis and in the middle of it pick up the jail again. He has put all the material about the jail together and simply interlarded the acts of the play with it. The play is almost as easy to read as if the other material were not there.

This play was the first book Mr. Faulkner published after he received the Nobel Prize. At the award ceremonies the speech he made was notably brief, less than a page in any of his books, and yet it may well outlive them all. "That singular swing to elevation" which Schopenhauer noted in great literature, is as marked in Faulkner's speech as it is absent from his writings. As he spoke he came back to what he called "the old universal truths, love and honor and pity and pride and compassion and sacrifice," from which he has wandered so far in his books. Without these, he said, a writer "writes not of love, but of lust." In what book ever did he himself write of love, and in how many books has he not written of lust? He went on to say that such a writer, one who has not learned "the old verities and truths of the heart," will deal with "defeats in which nobody loses anything of value, of victories without hope and worst of all without pity and compassion."

Many figures in his books throng to the mind with these words: Rosa Coldfield in *Absalom, Absalom!* and the final defeat of her death after a life of so little value that for forty-three years it had been only "a stubborn and amazed outrage"; Henry Sutpen's victory over Bon in the same book which brought him back to live "as if he were already a corpse; waking or sleeping it would be the same forever as long as he lived." These two can stand for all the victories and defeats Mr. Faulkner has recounted. No values are ever at stake; no victory ever brings hope or pity or compassion. Everything there is ends in futility. Darl says toward the end of *As I Lay Dying*: "How do our lives ravel out into the no-wind, no-sound, the weary gestures wearily recapitulant, echoes of old compulsions with no-hand on no-strings; in sunset we fall into furious attitudes, dead gestures of dolls." The passage deserves quoting not for itself but because it expresses Mr. Faulkner's creed. It could be matched over and over again in his books.

On the other side there is only courage. His characters are helpless. Their "every breath is a fresh cast with dice loaded against them," by "the dark diceman" who cares nothing for human anguish. Even so, they accept their inevitable doom with heads carried high. That is all.

In his speech Mr. Faulkner said that the writer's duty and privilege is to help men endure by lifting their hearts, not only by reminding them of what is good and great and enduring, but also by being a pillar of strength to them in their struggles toward it. In his books he reminds us only of the futility of all things human, and the certain defeat of all men's struggles. When he accepted the prize in those words of singular nobility and profound truth, he was pronouncing the condemnation of the work which had won him the prize.

The speech met with wide acclaim. It seemed to reveal depths he had never sounded before, and what he would do next was eagerly awaited. *Requiem for a Nun* was published in the following year. Its great importance comes from the fact that it was written after the speech.

Two women are the protagonists in the play, a Negro prostitute and murderer, and the girl who was a chief figure in *Sanctuary*, Temple Drake, grown up now and married. The thesis Mr. Faulkner sets forth is two-fold. One, the less prominent, is that old but terrible companion to so many religions, expiation. Sin can be expiated; the debt incurred thereby to God can be wiped out if the sinner suffers enough. Temple, induced to confess all the evil ever in her, says she has confessed for no purpose except to suffer: "Just suffering. Not for anything; just suffering. Just because it's good for you." Suffering as such is good, cleansing, powerful in itself to make white what was black. Temple must confess although her confession will do nothing for anybody: "We don't come here to save Nancy. What we came here for is just to give Temple Drake a good fair honest chance to suffer—just anguish for the sake of anguish."

This is the idea deepest in the Puritan ascetic, in all asceticism. Men of themselves can wipe out evil and achieve goodness if they are willing to torture themselves. They do not need forgiveness. "I have blotted out thy transgressions as a thick cloud and as a cloud thy sins: therefore return unto me." Mr. Faulkner's guilt-ridden men, curse-driven men, could never accept anything so full of pity and compassion, so natural in a Father to His children, as unearned forgiveness.

Expiation, however, plays a minor part in the play. The main thesis is that the end justifies the means—that ancient falsehood which has been the cause of the most hateful deeds men have done to each other. It is stated directly and clearly. Mr. Faulkner has dropped all his mannerisms. He tells the story as simply as possible, and his special gift of making an experience come alive has never been more strikingly shown. He needs no actors to carry over to his audience what he is telling them. They are not watching suffering people; they are suffering themselves, without any help from theatrical devices, almost it would seem, the dialogue is pitched so low, the language is so ordinary, without any help from the author.

In the last scene, which is in a prison the night before the Negro's execution, she and Temple talk to each other in brief sentences, the thought hardly expressed, the words completely commonplace, but intensity is there, rising, ever rising, through all they say.

And yet the text of this sermon Mr. Faulkner is preaching is not that a crime is pardonable, but that it is admirable, if it is seen by the criminal as the only way to stop another crime conceived of as greater. Nancy, the Negro, strangles Temple's six-month-old baby because she believes that the child's death will stop Temple from eloping with a blackmailer and a thief. Nancy is the nun who is lifted by her deed up to a level high above the others.

She has murdered a baby, with what Mr. Faulkner calls "that simple indeviable aim," and thereby she has become one with the saints and martyrs. Temple's friend and lawyer tells her that Nancy is dying "to prove that little children shall be intact, unanguished, untorn, unterrified." At the very end the odds are that she has saved Temple's soul too.

What has become of the great ideas in the Nobel Prize speech, "the old verities and truths of the heart, the old universal truths"? The lawyer's speech is the very acme of sentimentality. The play not only culminates in it, but is founded upon it. The danger which threatens all those who detest nature and escape from reality has dogged Mr. Faulkner always. In *Requiem for a Nun* it has overtaken him and overwhelmed him.

THE WAY
OF THE CHURCH

*An Address Given at the Church of St. John
Washington, D.C.*

My only claim to have anything to say which you might
wish to hear is that I have had a long acquaintance with the
classical world. So it is about the Greeks and Romans that
I am going to speak, about their relation to the young
Christian Church in its first beginnings. There lay before
the church in those earliest days two paths, the Greek way
and the Roman way. They were quite different. They did
not often connect. Inevitably the way of the church would
incline to one or the other because they were the two
great powers in the world she faced, each a great power,
but in a very different sense of the word. Rome was the
ruler of the civilized world; Greece was a little conquered
nation, an insignificant bit of the magnificent empire.
That was one point of view, but there was another. Spiritually, in the world of thought and art, Greece was the ruler.
The Romans acknowledged it. One of them writing in
those days said, "Captive Greece has taken captive her

conqueror." Nothing shows the Romans in a better light than that they recognized their own spiritual inferiority and set themselves to learn from a helpless, subject nation. Greece in her way was as great a power as Rome in the world where the Christian Church began.

Just at first she went the Greek way. The New Testament is written in Greek. The leaders of the little Christian centers—there was not yet one church—were men descended from Greeks or educated by Greeks. But that did not last long. She left the Greek way and turned to the Roman. It is easy to see why. In that world evil was so overwhelmingly powerful; it was most difficult to hold fast to the Christian faith that the only power which mattered, the only power which endured, was spiritual power. It seemed so feeble in face of the Roman Empire. But for generations the Greeks had been learning that the things that are seen are temporal. They had had to give up almost all they valued. Their freedom had been lost; their independence had been taken away; they were a poverty-stricken, subject country. One thing they had kept—their rule over men's spirits and minds. They had seen for themselves that riches, power, empire vanish, no matter how solidly founded, how mightily bulwarked, and only the splendor of the spirit endures. How well they had learned the lesson, their later writers show, especially the greatest, Plutarch. Might not the church if she had kept to the Greek way have turned away from temporal power? But she chose the Roman way.

In the darkness and among the dangers of that time the church at Rome was by far the most authoritative, also the strongest. And what were the Greeks? Thinkers and artists, the world called them. Thought and art are the products not of a powerful working force, a great mass of men acting together, but of separate, individual men going in their own different ways. People like that will never be dependably efficient. And yet somehow what they do lasts. The Roman Empire is gone. Greek art and thought are alive today, they have lasted more than three thousand years. In their very best days the Greeks could never make a Greek Empire. They did not care much about working together; they liked individual freedom. But to the Romans union was strength and that was what mattered. Minds and spirits—to the Romans they were fairly negligible. What was important was the will. When Christ said, "Seek and ye shall find," and "Ye shall know the truth and the truth will set you free," he said what was easy for a Greek to understand, but very hard for a Roman. They were wonderful organizers and an organization is not a place where people are encouraged to seek or to be free. The first essentials to the Romans were obedience to authority and disciplined control—as was natural to a nation which had been at war for eight hundred years. "Like a mighty army moves the Church of God." That is a Roman conception. There is not a word in Greek literature which praises unquestioning obedience or holds up doing and saying and thinking what everybody else does. The Greeks would have thought the first a matter for slaves not free men, and it would have been inconceivable to them that a man would think what others told him to.

So the young Christian Church turned from the Greek way and chose the Roman way. No more little scattered communities of Christians led by the spirit of truth which Christ had promised them. The Romans took them over and with their genius for organization built up one institution, so superbly planned and developed that it was finally able to step into the place of the Roman Empire. Never could that magnificent position have been reached by following the Greek way. The Roman way led the church to supreme power, power over heaven and hell as well as the earth.

All power tends to corrupt. Absolute power corrupts absolutely. The truth of Lord Acton's words has never been illustrated more clearly than by the medieval church. Corruption in the end weakens and kills. We do not today have to fear the power of any organized religion. But the church's rejection of the Greek way had results also which are still with us, which I believe are bad results from which the Greek way can help to free us.

I am going to speak only of three, but they are very important. The Romans thought very poorly of human nature. It was tolerable only when it was under strong control and properly hated when it got out of control and acted on its own. This was far from the Greek way. Socrates' fundamental conviction was that there was in every man a spark of good, a spark of the divine light, which could be kindled into a flame. As St. John, the Greek thinker among the Evangelists, was to say centuries later, "The true light which lighteth every man that cometh into the world." To make the spark blaze up in the souls of men was the object of Socrates' work which he called the service of God. In his speech to his judges just before they condemned him to death he said: "I will obey God rather than you, and as long as I have breath I will not cease from exhorting you, 'My Friend, are you not ashamed of caring so much about making money and about your reputation and your honours?' I shall reproach you for indifference to what is most valuable and prizing what is unimportant. I shall do this to everyone I meet, young and old, for this is God's command to me." He never told them what wisdom and truth were. All he did was to ask them questions, but his questions led them into the depths of themselves where he knew the spark could be found and kindled.

Plato repeated over and over again that the knowledge of God, the source of all good to men, could be reached because there was what he called "a kindred power in the soul." "Good," he said, "cannot be understood until we share something of it." Christ said that those who willed to do the will of God would know the doctrine, whether it be of God. The pure in heart can see Him. "The best man," Plato writes, "a gentle and noble nature who desires all truth and who seeks to be like God as far as that is possible for man, is the happiest man. He is a royal man, king over himself. Even when he is in poverty or sickness or any other seeming misfortune, all things will in the end work together for good to him in life and in death."

"Wherefore my counsel is that we hold fast ever to the heavenly way and follow after justice and excellence always, considering that the soul is immortal. Thus shall we live dear to one another and to the gods, both here and when, like conquerors in the games, we receive our reward."

To the Roman none of this was true. As he saw human nature it had nothing akin to the divine. This conception was taken over by the church. To be sure, the Jews who were the first Christians, knew that God had created man in His own image, but then there was the Fall and the end of human goodness. Humanity was evil throughout. The Greek belief did not wholly die as St. John's words about the true light show. St. Augustine, too, sometimes spoke Greek and not Latin, as when he said, "Thou hast made us for thyself and restless are our hearts until they rest in thee." But for one sentence like that in the early Christian Fathers, there are pages of invective against abominable human nature.

I believe that if the church had chosen the Greek way, some of the most terrible pages in history would never have had to be written. During the Middle Ages when the power of the church came near to being supreme, man's inhumanity to man was terrible. Cruelty was rampant—the Inquisition, the frightful prisons accused persons were flung into, the way they were tortured, the horrible ways the condemned were killed, the wholesale massacres, the way the Albigenses were treated, the Cathari, the Poor Men of Lyons. All this was certainly fostered and favored by the conviction that human nature was evil through and through and deserved all the suffering it could get. Around the year 1650 the Westminster Shorter Catechism was drawn up, a subject for reverential study in Presbyterian households for hundreds of years. (I learned it when I was a little girl.) In it this statement is made: "In Adam's fall mankind lost communion with God and are under His wrath and curse and so made liable to all the ills of this life, to death, and to the pains of hell forever." If God felt so toward everyone, certainly it was all right for man to make really objectionable people suffer as much as possible. Whatever they did it would be less than the pains of hell forever. Man certainly need not be more merciful and pitiful than God. If the church had taken the Greek way, that weight of human agony might never have been.

In Rome the influences were not for mercy and pity. Cicero, as kind a man as could be found there, writes a friend about some specially spectacular gladiatorial games he had been to: "They were magnificent. And yet what real pleasure can a cultivated person get watching a puny man being mangled by a tremendously powerful beast? Still, the games *are* an incomparable training in making the spectators despise suffering and death." But Athens never permitted the gladiatorial games, which to the rest of the world were the most delightful entertainment possible. Once when the Assembly was considering a proposal to have some gladiators come and stage one of their bloody contests, a man sprang up and cried, "Athenians, before we invite the gladiators come with me and tear down the temple to Pity." He won the day. They voted unanimously to refuse the gladiators. In all Athens' history only one man, Socrates, was put to death for his opinions, and even today we have not caught up with his executioners who killed him by giving him a poison that made him die with no pain.

My first point, then, is that by following the Greek way the church would have been more sensitive to suffering. The Inquisition might never have been.

The second point is that Socrates and Plato are a wonderful corrective to the danger which always threatens people when they unite into an institution with an avowed spiritual aim, the danger of formalism, of making the outside more important than the inside, of making a form of words, a theology, a more basic expression of the truth than what people do. Christ said, "Ye shall know them by their fruits"—not roots, but that is not the way the church went. The Inquisition put people to death not for living wickedly, but for making what to the Inquisitors were incorrect statements. The Greeks were not interested in trying to make correct statements about the infinite and the eternal. Plato said, "To find the father and maker of all is hard and having found him it is impossible to utter him."

In one of his letters written when he was very old, he said, "There is no way of putting it (the knowledge of God) into words. Acquaintance with it must come after a long period of dwelling upon it, when suddenly like a blaze kindled by a leaping spark, it is born in the soul." That flame shrivels up formalism. Socrates had his inner certainties, but he expressed them in his own way. In prison just before he died he said, as St. Paul was to say hundreds of years later, that the things that are seen pass away, the soul which is unseen is eternal. He added, "Let a man be of good cheer then who has arrayed his soul in her own jewels, which are justice and courage and nobility and truth—arrayed in these she is ready to go on her journey when her time comes." Just because he did not try to imprison the truth in a formula, his truth has lived. Here the Greek way can reinforce the Christian way. You will search the Gospels in vain for a definition of God. Christ never gave any. He called Him Our Father; he told the parable of the prodigal son; he said He would give the Holy Spirit to them that asked Him; he spoke of the love of God. But he never put into a definite statement what God is. It was the Roman way to make an authoritative statement about the things unseen and have it obediently accepted.

So my second point is, as Plato said, "the inadequacy of words to express the reality of the good which is God."

My third and last point is that the Greek way was not the easy way ever. "Excellence much labored for by the race of men," says Aristotle. "Long is the road thereto and rough and steep." Plato says, "Hard is the good." Christ said, "Straight is the gate and narrow is the way which leadeth unto life." It would be strange if the followers of Christ needed help from any Greek to make them realize that the way of Christ is not the easy way. Today, however, we are so comfortable here in this country, life is so much easier than it has ever been, tendencies are developing which make one feel anxious. There could hardly be a greater denial of the Christian way than to represent it as broad and smooth and leading to a happy success, but something very like that is being said nowadays. Against that idea Socrates and Plato stand immovable. It would have been inconceivable to them that a result of religion was a prosperous life. The only reward of serving God was to become able to serve Him better. Prosperity as a result of obeying God's command to him never entered Socrates' mind. In court when the sentence of death was pronounced, he told his judge, "I see clearly that the time has come when it is better for me to die, and so my accusers have done me no harm. Still—they did not mean to do me good and for this I may gently blame them. And now we go our ways, you to live and I to die. Which is better only God knows." A friend, who was with him in his prison cell when he drank the poison, told another, "I could not pity him. He seemed to me beyond that. I thought of him as blessed." Socrates had his reward.

A day or two before his death when Crito, who knew he could bribe jailers and free Socrates, came to him begging, "Let me save you, Socrates, your friends beseech you." Socrates said, "Dear Crito, a voice within me is telling me that I must not disobey my country's laws and do what is wrong in order to save my life. It is very loud, this voice, so that I can hardly hear another's. Yet if you wish to say more, speak and I will listen." "Socrates, I have nothing more to say." "Then leave me, Crito, to obey the will of God."

THIS I BELIEVE

*Written as a Radio Address for the Series
"This I Believe"*

Keats said, "I see in Shakespeare, the poet, the power of resting in uncertainty without any irritable reaching after fact and reason." What Shakespeare knew, he could not prove by fact and reason. In the truth he was seeking there could not be certainty, logically demonstrated or factually self-evident. There can never be that kind of certainty in the things that are greatest and most important to us. To me in the course of my long life, this has become a profound conviction. No facts, no reasoning, can prove to me that Beethoven's music is beautiful or that it is more blessed to give than to receive. No facts can prove to me that God is. There is an order of truth where we cannot have the proved certainties of the mind and where we do not need them. The search for spiritual truth may be hampered by them, not helped. When people are certain they know, the way to more knowledge is closed. But to perceive beauty opens the way to a fuller perception of beauty. To love goodness creates more goodness. Spiritual certainty leads to greater certainty.

The truths of the spirit are proved not by reasoning about them or finding explanations of them, but only by acting upon them. Their life is dependent upon what we do about them. Mercy, gentleness, forgiveness, patience—if we do not show them, they will cease to be. Upon us depends the reality of God here on the earth today. "If we love one another God dwelleth in us." Lives are the proof of the reality of God.

When the world we are living in is storm-driven and the bad that happens and the worse that threatens press urgently upon us, there is a strong tendency to emphasize men's baseness or their impotent insignificance. Is this the way the world is to go or not? It depends upon us.

St. John spoke of the true light that lighted every man coming into the world. Belief in the indestructible power of that light makes it indestructible. This lifts up the life of every man to an overwhelming importance and dignity.

God leaves us free. We are free to choose Him or reject Him. No tremendous miracle will come down from heaven to compel us to accept as a fact a Being powerful enough to work it. What would that kind of belief do toward making love or compassion a reality? God puts the truth of Himself into our hands. We must carry the burden of the proof, for His truth can be proved in no other way. "Glorious is the venture," Socrates said.

ROOTS OF
FREEDOM

Written as a Radio Address for the Voice of America Roots of Freedom Series

Freedom's challenge in the Atomic Age is a sobering topic. We are facing today a strange new world and we are all wondering what we are going to do with it. What are we going to do with one of our most precious possessions, freedom? The world we know, our Western world, began with something as new as the conquest of space.

Some 2,500 years ago Greece discovered freedom. Before that there was no freedom. There were great civilizations, splendid empires, but no freedom anywhere. Egypt, Babylon, Nineveh, were all tyrannies, one immensely powerful man ruling over helpless masses. In Greece, in Athens, a little city in a little country, there were no helpless masses, and a time came when the Athenians were led by a great man who did not want to be powerful. Absolute obedience to the ruler was what the leaders of the empires insisted on. Athens said no, there must never be absolute obedience to a man except in war. There must be willing obedience to what is good for all. Pericles, the great Athenian states-man, said: "We are a free government, but we obey the laws, more especially those which protect the oppressed, and the unwritten laws which, if broken, bring shame."

Athenians willingly obeyed the written laws which they themselves passed, and the unwritten, which must be obeyed if free men live together. They must show each other kindness and pity and the many qualities without which life would be intolerable except to a hermit in the desert. The Athenians never thought that a man was free if he could do what he wanted. A man was free if he was self-controlled. To make yourself obey what you approved was freedom. They were saved from looking at their lives as their own private affair. Each one felt responsible for the welfare of Athens, not because it was imposed on him from the outside, but because the city was his pride and his safety. The creed of the first free government in the world was liberty for all men who could control themselves and would take responsibility for the state. This was the conception that underlay the lofty reach of Greek genius.

But discovering freedom is not like discovering atomic bombs. It cannot be discovered once for all. If people do not prize it, and work for it, it will depart. Eternal vigilance is its price. Athens changed. It was a change that took place unnoticed though it was of the utmost importance, a spiritual change which penetrated the whole state. It had been the Athenians' pride and joy to give to their city. That they could get material benefits from her never entered their minds. There had to be a complete change of attitude before they could look at the city as an employer who paid her citizens for doing her work. Now instead of men giving to the state, the state was to give to them. What the people wanted was a government which would provide a comfortable life for them; and with this as the foremost object, ideas of freedom and self-reliance and responsibility were obscured to the point of disappearing. Athens was more and more looked on as a cooperative business possessed of great wealth in which all citizens had a right to share.

She reached the point when the freedom she really wanted was freedom from responsibility. There could be only one result. If men insisted on being free from the burden of self-dependence and responsibility for the common good, they would cease to be free. Responsibility is the price every man must pay for freedom. It is to be had on no other terms. Athens, the Athens of Ancient Greece, refused responsibility; she reached the end of freedom and was never to have it again.

But, "the excellent becomes the permanent," Aristotle said. Athens lost freedom forever, but freedom was not lost forever for the world. A great American statesman, James Madison, in or near the year 1776 A.D., referred to: "The capacity of mankind for self-government." No doubt he had not an idea that he was speaking Greek. Athens was not in the farthest background of his mind, but once a great and good idea has dawned upon man, it is never completely lost. The Atomic Age cannot destroy it. Somehow in this or that man's thought such an idea lives though unconsidered by the world of action. One can never be sure that it is not on the point of breaking out into action, only sure that it will do so sometime.

ADDRESS TO
THE ATHENIANS

*Delivered by Miss Hamilton in the Theatre of
Herodes Atticus at the Foot of the Acropolis
in 1957 on the Occasion of Her Being
Made a Citizen of Athens*

It is impossible for me to express my gratitude for the
honors shown me. I am a citizen of Athens, of the city I
have for so long loved as much as I love my own country.
This is the proudest moment of my life. And yet as I
stand here speaking to you under the very shadow of the
Acropolis a deeper feeling rises. I see Athens, the home of
beauty and of thought. Even today among buildings, the
Parthenon is supreme; Plato's thought has never been
transcended; of the four great tragedians, three are Greek.
We are here to see a performance of the *Prometheus*. In
all literature, Prometheus is the great rebel against tyranny.
It is most fitting that he should be presented to the world
now, in this period of the world's history, and here, in the
city of Athens. For Athens, truly the mother of beauty and
of thought, is also the mother of freedom. Freedom was a

Greek discovery. The Greeks were the first free nation in the world. In the *Prometheus* they have sent a ringing call down through the centuries to all who would be free. Prometheus, confronted with the utmost tyranny, will not submit. He tells the tyrant's messenger, who urges him to yield, "Go and persuade the sea-wave not to break. You will persuade me no more easily." That is the spirit Greece gave to the world. It challenges us and we need the challenge. Greece rose to the very height not because she was big, she was very small; not because she was rich, she was very poor; not even because she was wonderfully gifted. She rose because there was in the Greeks the greatest spirit that moves in humanity, the spirit that makes men free. It is impossible for us to believe that of all the nations of the world, Greece was the only one that had the vision of what St. John in the Gospels calls "the true light," which he adds, "lighteth every man who cometh into the world"; but we know that she was the only one who followed it. She kept on—on what one of her poets calls "the long and rough and steep road." Therefore her light was never extinguished. Therefore we are met tonight to see a play which has lived for 2,500 years. In those years the Greeks have been outstripped by science and technology, but never in the love of the truth, never in the creation of beauty and of freedom.